THE VALUE OF CONSERVATION?

A LITERATURE REVIEW OF THE ECONOMIC AND SOCIAL VALUE OF THE CULTURAL BUILT HERITAGE

THE VALUE OF CONSERVATION?

A LITERATURE REVIEW OF THE ECONOMIC AND SOCIAL VALUE OF THE CULTURAL BUILT HERITAGE

by
GERALD ALLISON, SUSAN BALL,
PAUL CHESHIRE, ALAN EVANS,
and MIKE STABLER

for
THE DEPARTMENT OF NATIONAL HERITAGE,
ENGLISH HERITAGE, and
THE ROYAL INSTITUTION OF CHARTERED SURVEYORS

ENGLISH HERITAGE

THE ROYAL
INSTITUTION
OF CHARTERED
SURVEYORS

© Copyright 1996 The Department of National Heritage, English Heritage,
and the Royal Institution of Chartered Surveyors
First published 1996 by English Heritage
21 Savile Row, London W1X 1AB

A catalogue record for this book is available from the British Library

ISBN 1 85074 658 3

Copy-edited and designed by C J Schüler

Contents

Foreword

Most of us believe that the conservation of the historic built environment makes a major contribution to the economic and social well-being of our towns and cities. Over the past fifty years, governments have successively strengthened both legislative protection and policy guidance on conserving our historic buildings and areas. PPG 15, *Planning and the historic environment,* published in September 1995, is the most recent example, and at the local level these policies are incorporated in statutory development plans. All of this reflects strong public support for the conservation of our cultural built heritage. However, while we are not short of opinions on the economic consequences of conservation, we are hampered by a lack of substantive evidence to support the assertion that, other than through encouraging tourism, conservation does contribute significantly to the economic well-being of our historic towns in particular. That is why we commissioned this research jointly from the Department of Economics at the University of Reading and DTZ Debenham Thorpe Property Consultants. The choice of the two organisations was intended to provide a depth and a balance, drawing together academic expertise and commercial awareness.

This literature review of the economic and social value of the conservation of the cultural built heritage marks the third stage of jointly sponsored research. In 1991 the RICS and English Heritage commissioned the Investment Property Databank (IPD) to provide a detailed study of the investment performance of listed commercial buildings. The results are now updated each year, and the results widely publicised in the property press, itself an encouraging indication of interest in historic buildings in commercial circles. The Department of National Heritage then joined English Heritage and the RICS for the second stage of research, in which the Department of Land Economy at the University of Cambridge considered the effect of listing on the value of buildings. The findings were of particular interest to building owners.

Each stage of research has contributed to our understanding, and further clarified the subject. We hope that with the publication of this report, others will take a stronger interest and look to develop their own understanding of the broad contribution which conservation of the historic environment makes to our towns and cities. We commend the work of the research teams, and look forward to the continuing discussion of their findings and recommendations.

THE RIGHT HONOURABLE
VIRGINIA BOTTOMLEY JP MP
Secretary of State for
National Heritage

SIR JOCELYN STEVENS CVO
Chairman, English Heritage

JEREMY BAYLIS
President , Royal Institution of
Chartered Surveyors

Executive summary

Introduction

1.1–1.12 This literature review marks the third stage of research jointly sponsored by the Royal Institution of Chartered Surveyors, English Heritage, and the Department of National Heritage. The brief was to identify issues for future research by the sponsors on the basis of a critical review of the methods which have been or can be used to measure, or value, the wider benefits to society of conserving historic buildings and areas.

The economists' and market views of conservation

2.1–2.6 Can conservation be left to the market? The problem is that the existence and preservation of a building or area are often valued most by people who are not the owners, who may neither live nor work there, or who may not even have been born yet. The costs of conservation fall on the existing owners, while some or most of the benefits accrue to others. The market may give opportunities for the latter to pay the former through a voluntary scheme such as the National Trust, but often this may not occur, and the market may fail.

2.7–2.12 This is why buildings are listed and conservation areas designated: to ensure their continued existence for those who would benefit now or in the future. Sometimes conservation may run with the grain of the market, when a residential conservation area is promoted by the residents, or a shopping street is kept attractive to shoppers. In these examples the interests of the owners coincide with those of the beneficiaries. In many other cases, however, conservation may run against market forces.

2.13–2.20 Conservation areas and historic properties form a relatively small part of the property market, and are subject to the wider influences on the market as a whole. In a depressed market, investment in the repair and maintenance of an individual historic property is unlikely to overcome the general trend; in a rising market there may be sufficient financial surplus to absorb the costs or physical limitations involved. Some commercial property owners have a generally negative view of conservation. Urban regeneration is an exception, but can be seen as a 'last ditch' solution to major economic difficulties requiring large-scale public investment.

Economic analysis: static and dynamic benefits

3.1–3.6 The benefits of most goods and services accrue to those who pay for them; what economists call 'externalities' are not usually considered important by the market.

But a building or area with architectural or historic character necessarily benefits others: apart from the direct use value which benefits those who own or occupy the buildings, there is also an indirect use value which benefits those who pass the buildings or visit the area. In this way, tourists who visit historic towns and cities such as Bath benefit from the visit, even if they spend no money. In addition there are also, more nebulously, option value and existence value. People may benefit from the option to visit somewhere, even if they never exercise the option. They may also benefit from the continued existence of a building which they may never visit, so that reports of environmental damage to the Taj Mahal, for example, may affect the enjoyment of people who would never visit it.

3.7–3.26 Conservation of buildings and areas may also have dynamic effects. The improvement or maintenance of a building or buildings may cause the price or rent of nearby buildings to rise, so revitalising the economy of the area. Here again market forces may not produce a result which is socially and economically desirable in the long run.

Valuing the urban environment

4.1–4.8 How can one value those benefits produced by urban conservation that are not reflected directly in the prices of the buildings conserved? A number of methods have been suggested which would allow authorities to take into account the 'externalities' associated with different conservation decisions. The concern here, however, is to try to estimate the economic value of urban environments with as much certainty as possible. The three methods most likely to be used are called the Hedonic Pricing Method, the Travel Cost Method, and the Contingent Valuation Method. Though they can be used for valuing characteristics of either the urban or the natural environment, almost all studies have been concerned with the latter.

4.9–4.12 The Hedonic Pricing Method (HPM) uses changes in the value of property to estimate the value of environmental goods: not just the properties that are directly conserved, but also those that are indirectly affected. Most studies are concerned with residential property, however, and practically none with commercial buildings. There is a significant body of research into the value of architectural styles and of conservation area designation, although this is based on US practice.

4.13–4.14 The Travel Cost Method (TCM) is based on the premise that visitors reveal the value they put on a site by the amount they are willing to spend in travelling to it.

This method has been much used to value recreational facilities in rural areas, but has been virtually unused in assessing the value of urban facilities. Because many chose to live in or near conserved areas, the Travel Cost Method has a rather limited applicability to valuing urban conservation.

4.15–4.21 The Contingent Valuation Method (CVM) relies on using questionnaires to ask people to declare the value they put on environmental goods. This method has been developed considerably in recent years. It has been used to value natural environmental goods and, in one significant urban case, the existence of Durham Cathedral. The literature review suggests that this is probably the most suitable method for development to value the benefits of urban conservation, but benchmarking studies need to be undertaken in an urban context to compare values estimated using CVM methods with those derived from other methods.

Literature review of cases

5.1–5.15 The review of cases reported in the literature review, including material from public bodies and leading academic journals, confirmed that there is as yet relatively little material other than anecdotal evidence to support or refute the hypothesis that conservation practices bring dynamic benefits to society. A market belief that conservation can be a constraint was expressed. The cases reviewed are not a balanced sample, and there continues to be a shortage of factual analysis. Few case studies have attempted to assess the multi-faceted outcomes of conserving the cultural built heritage, and these are confined to instances where enhancement of the built environment had aimed, and was largely agreed to have helped, to stimulate investment and regeneration.

5.16 A synthesis of case studies suggests that conclusions must remain general because:

- the socio-economic externalities of the conservation of the cultural built heritage are seldom examined in any degree of detail

- 'conservation' is an imprecise term which cannot easily be subjected to rigorous analysis

5.17 Nonetheless, it is possible to suggest four potentially contrasting scenarios:

- investment in conservation creates employment

- the revitalisation of the cultural heritage brings a mixture of costs and benefits

- conservation is an important means by which people maintain their socio-cultural identity, and has the potential to improve perception of an area

- the cultural built heritage takes a decisive share in the dispersed economic flows from tourism

5.18–5.23 There is a range of tools for evaluation, set out in the report, but at present there is also a lack of rigorous case analysis. This reflects a general reluctance to provide publicly accessible data, in spite of the fact that investment in the heritage often involves a partnership of different interests.

Conclusions and issues for research

6.1–6.9 In assessing the static benefits of urban conservation, the Contingent Valuation Method is likely to be the most successful, but the Hedonic Pricing Method is also relevant. An important issue for research is the extent to which people derive a sense of place from, and so attach value to, the outward appearance of groups of buildings, rather than their intrinsic qualities and integrity.

6.10–6.11 The dynamic benefits of investing in conservation are likely to be subject to a high degree of risk and uncertainty. This is in itself an argument, on the insurance principle, for public involvement in funding. Are the long-term returns likely to be better than the short-term, in that investors may be able to capture more of the benefits of conservation? If so, how can this influence the mechanisms for investment in historic areas?

6.12–6.18 There is a need for detailed and objective case studies undertaken with the explicit aim of exploring the benefits of conservation. This should take place within a conceptual economic framework such as Cost-Benefit Analysis (suitably adapted and developed, as in Community Impact Analysis), which conceptually clarifies the nature of the benefits, and separates distribution effects. Specific issues to be addressed include:

- what, if any, role is played by 'anchor' buildings?

- what contribution to entrepreneurship can restored residential, commercial, and industrial areas make?

- what is the minimum scale of effective action?

- what scale of conservation is required to generate a potential for the development of satisfying urban lifestyles which, in turn, reinforce the success of the initial conservation effort by attracting new residents and businesses to serve those residents?

- is the mix of buildings critical in this process?

- what role does the image of a city play in its regeneration?

- how can conservation contribute to that image?

- what is the most effective administrative structure?

- what is the most effective funding mechanism?

- how much private investment does a given expenditure of public funds attract?

- are there factors which systematically influence the amount of private investment attracted by public funding?

- what is the most useful information which can be collected from grant recipients to enable effective assessment of the impact of public investment in urban conservation?

6.19 There is no present answer, in a numeric sense, to the question, 'What are the dynamic benefits of urban conservation?' It is certain, however, that they can be large and positive (although this is not the case in all circumstances). The best way to address the question is probably through detailed and structured case studies, since data do not, and in sufficient quantity could not, exist for econometric studies. Such case studies should be informed by an understanding of how the economic benefits should be defined, include examples of unsuccessful as well as of successful cases, and attempt not only to identify the overall contribution of conservation, but also to examine more specific questions, including those listed above. In addition, the awarding of conservation- related grants should, in appropriate cases, be made conditional on the provision of data which would be used to evaluate the benefits of conservation.

Chapter 1 Introduction

1.1 The socio-cultural value of our architectural heritage, and the economic impact of urban conservation and historic centre recovery, are matters of concern to a widening audience. The need to assess conservation issues has recently been brought to the fore by the Secretary of State for National Heritage, through the publication of a consultation paper, *Protecting our heritage*, in May 1996. This will follow the issue of PPG 15, *Planning in the historic environment*, in September 1994, the Government's first conservation policy statement in seven years. Beyond England, the Council of Europe has considered the economic aspects of policies for the conservation of the cultural built heritage at the IVth European Conference of Ministers Responsible for the Cultural Heritage, held in Helsinki in 1996.

1.2 The need to understand the value of conservation is also recognised by English Heritage, the Department of National Heritage, and the Royal Institution of Chartered Surveyors (RICS), who have commissioned the present study aimed at obtaining a better understanding of the issues and principles involved.

1.3 It represents the latest step in a cooperative study which originated in 1991, when the RICS organised four half-day seminars to bring together property owners and professionals with planners and senior representatives from English Heritage. The objective was to encourage greater mutual understanding, and to foster the use of both commercial and specialist conservation skills to secure a long-term future for problematic listed buildings. At their conclusion, 11 points were agreed, including a commitment to further research.

1.4 In the first stage of this research, the Investment Property Databank (IPD) analysed its unrivalled records in order to assess the investment performance of listed commercial buildings in relation to other specific categories and the market as a whole (IPD 1993). The IPD concluded that listed commercial buildings held in portfolios by investing institutions had steadily out-performed unlisted ones over the long term, though they may do less well over short periods of change such as the last recession. The RICS and English Heritage have since sponsored the annual updating of this research. The IPD report of February 1995 stated that

listed office buildings in England and Wales... held as investments by the major financial institutions, have exhibited performance trends which have not differed dramatically from those of other office development.

The 1996 update reported that, in the longer term, listed buildings still outperform other office categories by a significant margin (IPD 1996).

1.5 The sponsors of the research were aware that the buildings in IPD's databank were not necessarily typical of listed commercial buildings, since their selection by the major financial institutions would have required that they were, or were rapidly anticipated to become, useable, lettable, suitably located, and in reasonable condition. The probable lack of typicality of the IPD sample of listed buildings led to a second stage of research, jointly sponsored by the RICS, English Heritage, and the Department of National Heritage. This was undertaken by the University of Cambridge's Department of Land Economy (Scanlon *et al* 1994), which set out to test the hypothesis that

restrictions imposed by listing affect the market value of listed buildings, and that the magnitude and direction of this effect varies according to the location and type of building.

1.6 In essence, the research undertaken by the Department of Land Economy focused on the effect of listing on value. The Department used a number of case studies, the value of which was reduced by the poor quality of available information on property valuations, and the limits imposed on access to this information (full studies were undertaken on 11 properties at the margin of economic viability). The conclusions should therefore be treated with caution.

1.7 The case studies suggested that the capital value of commercial buildings is likely to be reduced at the time of listing, since listing is likely to limit future changes to the building. For most listed buildings such a reduction is itself now a matter of history, however. A conference was held in May 1994 to discuss the results of this second stage of research. Discussion focused on the generally accepted view that although listing, or inclusion in a conservation area, may impose a cost on the owner of an affected building, there may be wider benefits to society at large which at least equal the individual loss. Indeed, conservation legislation and policy are predicated on that assumption.

1.8 As a result, the RICS, English Heritage, and the Department of National Heritage jointly commissioned the present study, with the intention of bringing the academic expertise of the Department of Economics, University of Reading, and the commercial awareness of DTZ Debenham Thorpe jointly to bear on the issue. The study brief required that issues for future research should be identified on the basis of a literature review of existing work in the field. The hope was, and remains, to develop methods which can be used to understand better the wider benefits of conserving historic buildings and areas, and to place some form of value on those benefits. The benefits might then be compared with the more easily measured costs of individual projects.

1.9 The literature review examines the methods that have been used to measure the benefits (and costs) of conservation, drawing on work concerned with the natural as well as the built environment, and examines their suitability for future use. In this report, 'conservation' is taken in a wide context. It is not limited to activity in the UK, or to those buildings or areas which are the subject of statutory protection. Instead the report looks at instances where positive action has been taken to continue and enhance the use of buildings or areas which have been considered to be of some cultural as well as economic value.

1.10 The work undertaken by the University of Reading and DTZ Debenham Thorpe had several stages. An interim report was presented to a consultation held at the King's Manor, University of York, in February 1995 (Stabler 1995), the proceedings of which also include reflections on the emerging issues by Paul Drury of English Heritage (Drury 1995, 22–4). Following the completion of the literature review, a workshop was held on 29 March 1995 with an invited group to discuss the early results. A public seminar held in London on 9 June 1995 saw the presentation of drafts of the papers included in this report, and played an important part in refining them for publication. A summary of proceedings at the seminar forms Appendix 3.

1.11 The study is limited to a review of existing literature in the UK, Europe, and the USA. It aims to establish:

• the extent to which this important topic has already been assessed

• the extent to which there is an understanding of the economic and social values created by conservation practice

• what methods exist for the measurement of these values

The study explores the published literature, seeking an analysis of the experiences of governments, owners, occupiers, and investors in property, together with the views and analysis of schemes by planning authorities, development corporations, and developers in the UK, Europe, and North America.

1.12 This report brings together the literature reviews carried out by the University of Reading and by DTZ Debenham Thorpe. As was to be expected, the two research establishments have considered the nature of the problem in different ways using different approaches. The economists at the University of Reading have been particularly concerned with work on social and economic valuation of the urban environment and, more exactly, with the benefits which 'consumers' derive from the existence and preservation of particular buildings or areas. Since the concern is with valuation at a point in time, this approach could be categorised as static. DTZ Debenham Thorpe, on the other hand, has been particularly concerned with the interaction between the conservation of properties and the local economy, reflected through the property market in, for example, the contribution of conservation to urban regeneration projects. Since this approach involves the observation of changes over time, it could be characterised as dynamic.

1.13 Chapter 2 sets out the economic reasons why conservation cannot necessarily be left to the market, and the market view of conservation. In Chapter 3, the economic analysis of both the static and the dynamic approaches is described. Chapter 4 surveys the literature relating to the valuation of the urban environment (the static approach), and in Chapter 5 case studies identified in the literature review are considered (the dynamic approach). Chapter 6 sets out conclusions and recommendations for future lines of research.

Chapter 2 The economists' and market view of conservation

Introduction

2.1 This chapter examines the academic literature in the discipline of economics which points to the reasons why conservation cannot necessarily be left to the market. It then goes on to outline market perceptions of conservation policies.

The economists' view of conservation

2.2 Adam Smith's remarks regarding the way in which, in a market economy, there is a hidden hand causing individuals' actions to lead to maximum efficiency are well known. Less well known has been the work of numerous less famous economists in the ensuing two hundred years, who have attempted to specify the conditions under which Smith's argument holds, and those under which it does not. Some conditions were known to, and remarked on by, Smith himself, for example the dangers of monopolies and industrial cartels. Some have become clearer over the years. In the context of the value of urban conservation, the important point is this: a market will work efficiently to maximise welfare provided that the price paid for a good is an accurate representation of its value to society. This would certainly be true in situations where the good being purchased is to be wholly owned and consumed by a person who is the sole beneficiary of its particular attributes. The examples given by economists are often items of food, since the purchase and consumption of, say, an apple clearly benefits that consumer, and it is difficult to see how, in normal circumstances, its consumption might benefit anyone else.

2.3 In many cases, purchase and consumption is organised within a group. The clearest and most frequent example is the purchase of items for family consumption. A subscription to cable television, for example, presumes that the total value of the good to all members of the family together is equal to the price paid. Once again, in these circumstances, the market economy works to achieve maximum efficiency. However, it has to be recognised that there may be things which have to be consumed by groups which, unlike a family, have no voluntary mechanism to ensure that the price paid is equal to the collective valuation. One example of such a good, it has long been recognised, is defence, and so nations collect through the taxation system to pay for it. Between goods for public or collective consumption, such as defence, and private goods, such as food, are many other goods whose consumption or ownership by one person affects the welfare of others. To maximise efficiency in these circumstances, in theory, the price paid for the good should be equal to the total estimate of its value by all those affected by its consumption.

Of course in most cases the effects on those other than the owner may be minimal, and can safely be ignored. For example, the flowers in a household's front garden may give pleasure to passers-by, but it is unlikely that any contribution that they might make to the household growing the flowers would alter, other than marginally, what was grown. The price they would pay for the pleasure they enjoyed would simply not be big enough. In other cases these 'external' effects may be deliberately minimised — for example, a person's record player may voluntarily be played at a level which does not disturb other people (and, if it is not, sanctions of one kind or another may be imposed to ensure that it is). Nevertheless, in some circumstances these external effects may be important, and if they are ignored, markets left to operate without any form of policy intervention will not achieve the level of efficiency which Smith perceived. Economists have long referred to this problem by the technical term of 'market failure'. Put simply, the benefits and the costs are not borne by the same people.

2.4 This may be so in the case of land and buildings. Those who pass by a house or through an area cannot be made blind to its attractiveness (or ugliness) nor, entirely, to its historical associations. Architecture, by its nature, cannot be made into an art form which is only for private consumption, as can painting or music. It cannot avoid affecting the welfare of people other than its owner. Sometimes this effect is deliberate: a building, for example Buckingham Palace, may be designed to make a statement about the character of the owner, or in the case of churches (for example York Minster) the implied owner. Sometimes, however, the effect is almost accidental: in the case of almost any Cotswold village, for example Castle Combe, the value of the buildings to those who do not own them is unintended by the owners, but still substantial.

2.5 In these circumstances the market price, for maximum welfare (ie for Adam Smith's invisible hand to work efficiently), should, as has already been indicated, be equal to the sum of the value put on the existence of the building or buildings by all those who have any interest, including the owner or occupier. The problem is that the value attached by those other than the owner or occupier may be substantial, and therefore cannot be neglected as insignificant. Those interested others are of course both many and difficult to identify, but sometimes institutions can participate in the market on their behalf. The most important of these institutions in the private sector in Britain is the National Trust, which seeks, through voluntary effort and financing, to buy or own and preserve buildings on behalf of all those who have an interest, both now and in the future.

2.6 In most circumstances, however, the market participation of institutions such as the National Trust is difficult or unlikely, both because their resources are not great enough and because the value of the building to those other than the owner, although significant, is not of national importance. In these circumstances, various facets of the town planning system can be used to try to ensure that the actions of the owner do not reduce the welfare of others. In most cases town planning controls are used where aesthetic implications are minimal, and where the actions of the owners of land can affect the welfare of those owning, occupying or living on land nearby. Daylighting standards can be preserved, densities controlled, parking spaces required, non-conforming uses prohibited, pollution controlled or open space and environmentally sensitive sites preserved. In all developed countries, some form of town planning controls has come to be seen as necessary because of the way that the use of land and buildings by the owners and occupiers affects other members of society. What has happened, therefore, is that town planning controls are used to preserve buildings and areas which are considered to be of aesthetic or cultural importance, whose use or alteration would significantly affect others, sometimes neighbours, sometimes those not resident in the area. In this way, the valuations put on the continued use and maintenance of a particular area or building by these others may be taken into account when determining the form of its existence.

Conservation and controls

2.7 To improve on the kind of property use that would result from the unrestrained operation of the market, however, controls must not be arbitrary. Their use must be predicated by a presumption that the total social value created is equal to the cost imposed on the economy or the owner or occupier. In other words, the value put on the conservation of a building or an area should be at least equal to the cost of preserving it. However, the cost to society of conservation can largely be measured by the cost of opportunities forgone because the site cannot be developed or redeveloped. This in turn may be measured by the difference between the value of the building and its site subject to normal planning controls, and its value with opportunities for development constrained by additional conservation controls, an issue which was explored by the research commissioned from the University of Cambridge (Scanlon *et al* 1994).

2.8 Thus the costs will be borne by the owner at the time of listing, the benefits will often accrue primarily to the rest of society, and the condition for efficiency implies that these gains must be greater than the cost to the owner. In some cases the owner may also benefit, largely because the conservation of other buildings in the area will preserve the value of all the properties. In some cases, such as residential areas of high architectural quality, this condition may easily be seen to be satisfied, because the residents, taken as a whole, gain more from the preservation of their environment than they lose from the restrictions imposed on them. The residents may all be in favour, indeed may advocate the designation of their neighbourhood as a conservation area. In such cases it is obvious that the total benefits must outweigh the total costs. The problem of market failure that conservation has to solve is a simple one stemming from the interdependence of decision-making for owners of neighbouring properties. What is in the collective interest of all the group together is not in the individual interest of any owner in isolation.

2.9 It is also possible that a group of shops forming a harmonious ensemble which is attractive to customers could be designated as a conservation area. This may be supported by their owners on the grounds that the increase in the value of their shops resulting from the certainty of environmental conservation outweighs any possible gains they might make from redevelopment. The same may be true for individual shops which might gain from the trade attracted to a residential area by its environmental attributes. The retail activities, public houses, tea shops, and hotels in Cotswold villages form an obvious example. Furthermore, as the research undertaken by the University of Cambridge and IPD (1996) suggested, the location of commercial properties plays a substantial role in determining their value.

2.10 This may sometimes be true of offices as well, especially in locations such as an eighteenth-century square or the market place of an old country town. The owner of each building, considered in isolation, might increase the value of his or her site by redeveloping it, but the designation of the area as a whole could attract tenants who are collectively prepared to pay higher rents than those which would be realised if individual sites were redeveloped. This is a supposition that would need to be tested empirically. It is possible that major occupiers would simply move elsewhere because the premises were no longer suitable.

2.11 Establishing whether the gains outweigh the losses in such cases is more problematic. There is evidence that some occupiers may perceive advantages in conservation. The offices of architects and quantity surveyors, for example, will often be found in listed buildings or small conservation areas outside the main commercial districts of a city. Presumably they consider such an environment commercially advantageous, and the image of the building influences their choice. It is possible that higher rents may be charged and that gains accruing to the owners and occupiers outweigh the costs, but again this is an assertion requiring investigation.

2.12 In the case of many listed buildings and conservation areas, however, the benefits of conservation will not accrue mainly — or even at all — to the owners or the occupiers, but to the rest of society. In these circumstances there has to be some way in which the benefits to society can be measured.

The property market's view of conservation

2.13 Conservation property is a small part of the property market, but one which consumes substantial investment from both public and private sectors. Value is normally generated by a demand for certain physical characteristics such as location, design, and condition, rather than by conservation designations, although designation is important because it limits the options.

2.14 The property market is not consistent. Demand and values change as a result of a range of factors, but largely in response to the national economy. It is a market of peaks and troughs; its cycles are an exaggerated reflection of the national economy. In such a market, the true economic value of conservation property will inevitably be influenced and distorted by market trends beyond the individual characteristics of the property itself. In a depressed property market, investment in an individual property is not likely to overcome the general trend, but in a rising market there may be sufficient financial surplus to absorb the additional costs or physical limitations of a conservation property.

2.15 Conservation properties can form part of sites where demolition and redevelopment could deliver the greatest market value, and in some cases such value can overwhelm current use value of the property. This defines a conflict between conservation and the market, since the fact that the residual value of the site of some listed buildings would be greater if the building were demolished and redeveloped, rather than put to the most beneficial use consistent with the conservation of its special architectural or historic interest, has never been accepted as a valid argument for granting consent for demolition.

2.16 Most owners of commercial buildings regard their property simply as a unit of production whose only purpose is to support business functions at the lowest possible cost. The economic efficiency of the building is the predominant consideration, and the owner would ideally wish to be entirely free to redevelop or adapt buildings to improve production, before disposing of the property at its maximum value, including redevelopment potential, when it no longer plays a useful part in the business.

2.17 Owners of commercial buildings wish to keep expenditure on property to a minimum. Any additional costs arising from a need to maintain to a higher standard or retain a building because of conservation issues will be unwelcome. Although such maintenance costs may be a relatively small proportion of total occupancy costs, they may be seen by the owners or occupiers as a 'tax' to pay for public benefits.

2.18 Some property owners hold large estates of conservation property. They are seen by the market as specialists in a development 'niche'. Invariably such owners are making the most of existing historic assets, and there is little evidence of a substantial commercial market specifically for conservation property alone.

2.19 The sudden listing of a building considered to be approaching the end of its useful economic life, when the market would tend to be contemplating demolition and redevelopment, is obviously considered unwelcome by many property owners, since it may prevent or delay the anticipated financial returns from development or disposal. This issue came to the fore during the public consultation period on the post-war industrial and commercial buildings proposed for listing in 1995.

2.20 The resistance of some commercial property owners to conservation policies, and in particular to the listing of buildings, may be set in the context of a common belief that this obstructs the normal recycling of properties that are no longer physically suited to occupier demand, and which are not obviously adaptable for continued use. There is a general perception by some commercial property owners that conservation policies are a negative rather than a positive policy. Urban regeneration is an exception, but can be seen by the market as a 'last ditch' solution to major economic difficulties requiring large-scale public investment.

Chapter 3 Economic analysis: static and dynamic benefits

Introduction

3.1 This chapter sets out a conceptual framework for viewing the benefits of conservation. It is not put forward as definitive, but rather suggested as a possibly useful means of identifying the benefits of conservation.

Static benefits

3.2 Although the non-priced elements of conservation have been emphasised, it must not be forgotten that the properties and land involved are traded in the market, where excludability can normally be exercised; that is to say, the benefits can be confined to the purchaser rather than extended to a wider group. In the market, the exchange value of a good or service is indicated by the price at which it is traded. Nevertheless, it is recognised in economics that the use value can be greater than this for all but the marginal consumer, on the assumption of a demand curve sloping downward from left to right, as there are many purchasers who are willing to pay a price above that which prevails in the market. This is known as consumers' surplus, which yields an aggregate use value above the sum of the price paid by individual consumers and the quantity purchased by each. In practice, the concept of consumers' surplus is rarely invoked to ascertain the total user value of priced goods, but it is of interest because it forms the theoretical foundation of a valuation method for establishing the willingness to pay for non-priced goods.

3.3 As already shown, market prices are a poor indicator of the value of many public or collective consumption goods, because their key feature consists of the many externalities which are not taken account of in the price for which the goods are sold. This is the case for the majority of environmental goods, such as unique natural and historic human-made resources, which fall into a category for which market values are not available. This arises, essentially, because they are open access or common property resources. Accordingly, even where they are in private ownership, property rights cannot be exercised because consumers cannot be prevented from using them. In economic terms, they have the characteristics of non-exclusion, and as a consequence the owners or suppliers are unable to charge a price. This has two effects. First, they may not be supplied in sufficient quantities to meet demand, as owners have no incentive to do so, and second, they may be overused simply because demand is greater than it would be if consumers were required to pay for them; price would ration demand.

3.4 Although many collective consumption goods remain unmeasured and unpriced, their true value can be considered to be much greater than their market price because they are unique. Overuse of them may initiate an irreversible trend which will lead to their destruction, and because they are unique, they cannot be reproduced. This often imparts a non-use, or passive, value, in addition to the user benefits. Such goods therefore have a value which transcends both their exchange value (any price paid) and their user value (the consumers' surplus). In the context of environmental and collective consumption goods, a number of non-user benefits or values have been identified which should be added to the user values to yield what is known as Total Economic Value (TEV).

3.5 With respect to static benefits, which are generated at one point in time and arise from existing resources such as historic buildings and public spaces (in effect from the stock of resources in their present state), the following are generally, although not universally, accepted by economists as relevant kinds of value:

• *option value* This is the potential benefit which consumers might derive from resources. It is an expression of a willingness to pay for their preservation in order to retain the option of using them in the future. In this sense option demand is a quasi-use value. It may be extended to include an option for others to enjoy the consumption of certain resources, a kind of vicarious demand. Some economists distinguish between demand by the current and by future generations. The term bequest value has been coined to suggest the value which the present generation places on resources, when it expresses a willingness to pay for their preservation for the benefit of future generations. This, however, can be construed as a form of option demand, and is viewed as such here.

• *intrinsic or existence value* This is a more complex and unclear form of value, in that it can be considered to be unrelated to demand. People may have preferences for, and therefore place value on, the continued existence of resources which they have no intention of ever using. Therefore the preservation of both natural and human-made resources may be advocated because it is recognised that they have intrinsic value.

3.6 Thus, with regard to historic buildings and conservation areas, it is possible to perceive them in the same way as the natural environment, as possessing Total Economic Value (TEV) consisting of:

• user value, both direct and indirect; for example, the occupation and use of a historic building would represent direct value, while its appearance, which gives pleasure to occupiers, the local community at large, and visitors, would constitute indirect value.

- option value, which encompasses potential use by an individual or that individual's preference for use by others or by future generations. Thus there would be a willingness to pay to retain the possibility of visiting a conserved area or building. For example, potential tourists might be willing to pay to prevent Exeter Cathedral from being demolished.

- non-use value, essentially existence value, whereby people might be willing to pay something simply to know a building or area was going to be conserved, even though they expect never to visit it. This would mainly be relevant in the case of world landmarks such as the Tower of London, but may also be relevant for whole historic city centres or public urban spaces such as Oxford, Bath, or the city of Venice. More problematic is the possibility that a value is placed on conservation *per se* — that one might be willing to pay something simply to know that a reasonable number of moderately interesting nineteenth-century districts are to be conserved.

So TEV = use value + option value + existence value.

While use value is relevant to the majority of conservation properties, option and non-use value are more likely to apply to national monuments than to the more typical listed buildings.

Dynamic benefits

3.7 So far the analysis has been based on the implicit assumption that the world is fixed — there is a given heritage of buildings and townscape, and the relevant question is 'what value do people attach to heritage?' In addition to this question of the current value of heritage, however, there is what may be called the 'dynamic' question. Is it possible that conservation may have a beneficial effect in causing or accelerating urban regeneration? If that does prove to be the case, then it is not sufficient simply to estimate the size of a given (if mainly invisible) pie; urban (or indeed historic landscape) conservation may act as a catalyst in making the pie bigger.

3.8 This argument derives ultimately from a seminal contribution by Davis and Whinston (1961) to the analysis of urban renewal. They pointed out that, in an urban context, individuals pursuing their own interests and reacting to market prices will systematically tend to underinvest in the maintenance of their properties. Since this process is dynamic, it will tend to generate competitive underinvestment by neighbours, which will reduce the life of buildings. Consequently, this form of dynamic market failure will lead to the progressive deterioration of the whole urban environment. Slum areas will come into existence, and remain in existence because no owners will find it worthwhile to renovate their properties.

3.9 This comes about, Davis and Whinston argued, because of the interdependence of the value of a house and that of its neighbours. Although expenditure on maintenance and upkeep, other things being equal, increases the value of a specific house, it also increases the value of neighbouring properties. It follows that neglect of a property reduces the value of neighbouring dwellings. Rational property owners wishing to maximise profits over time will adopt a strategy of undermaintaining their property relative to neighbouring properties. Overmaintenance will not be worthwhile, because the expenditure would not increase the value of the property, since this will largely be determined by the condition of the neighbouring properties. Thus, because of the interdependence of seemingly rational decisions by individual owners and the values of neighbouring properties, housing areas may go into near-terminal decline. Accordingly, as indicated in the original Davis and Whinston article, public intervention would be justified in order to secure the maintenance of values or to bring about urban renewal.

3.10 The Davis and Whinston argument can, however, be put into reverse. If the value of a property is negatively affected by the physical characteristics of the surrounding buildings, then it also follows that the value of surrounding buildings may be positively affected by the physical characteristics of a property or properties. Thus if conservation results in an improvement in the physical characteristics of a building, this may be a partial trigger for urban regeneration.

3.11 The processes of generating environmental improvement and the change in the social character of an area may be interdependent. What one might call the reverse Davis and Whinston argument therefore implies that the conservation and improvement of a group of buildings will result in higher rents and prices being obtained. Moreover, this will have beneficial spillover effects on property values and rents in the surrounding locations, perhaps altering their social character as well.

3.12 These neighbourhood effects, moreover, can equally well be applied to buildings used for commercial and other purposes as well as housing. Indeed, some effects may be more far-reaching and elusive, but no less important, than those analysed by Davis and Whinston in the more prosaic context of slum creation or urban renewal. For example, by investing in conservation policies for architecturally significant buildings or areas, public agencies may encourage the owners of adjoining properties to upgrade them. The improved environment might encourage people with new skills to move into the area, or persuade skilled people to remain. They in turn might encourage new businesses to locate in the conserved buildings and areas, which would facilitate the emergence of new business opportunities, additional spending, and the creation of yet more businesses.

3.13 It seems plausible to assume that the value put on the environment is not only positively related to rises in income, but also increases more than proportionately with them. In economic terms, environmental preference is a superior good. So, for example, the Roskill Commission on the third London airport found many years ago that the value of more expensive houses was likely to depreciate by proportionately more at any given noise level than the value of less expensive houses. Furthermore, there is evidence that wealthier households prefer, and can afford, to live in proximity to other wealthier households. It follows, therefore, that wealthier households will probably live in neighbourhoods with better physical environments and at lower densities, in houses of a better physical and architectural quality. This is not invariably so, as other characteristics, such as location, might make specific properties unsuitable for occupation by the better-off.

3.14 While recognising this, it can nevertheless be posited that — other things being equal — the higher the architectural quality of a house and of an area, the more likely it is to be occupied by someone with a higher income. In this connection, the listing of an individual building has two effects. In the first place the value of the building itself may be reduced because the way in which it can be altered is constrained. This result depends on a fundamental mathematical and economic theorem: the value achieved subject to constraints cannot be increased, but may be reduced, by the imposition of a further constraint. It follows that listing as such does not increase a building's value. On the other hand, the designation of an area surrounding a building as a conservation area may increase the value of the building if that area is regarded as worth conserving, for reasons discussed in paragraph 2.8. The freedom of manoeuvre of the other owners is now reduced. They cannot do things to their properties which would cause the value of other properties to deteriorate by allowing the environment to deteriorate.

3.15 Thus designation as a conservation area on the whole raises the value of properties because the physical environment surrounding them becomes more secure and more likely to be realisable on any future sale of individual properties. It follows that designation of a residential quarter as a conservation area, if it is not already occupied by higher income households, and provided the environment is regarded as being worthy of conservation, will almost certainly lead to some 'gentrification', as higher income groups regard their investment as both worthwhile and secure. Since maintenance of such properties will be better, the result is also likely to be some improvement in the physical characteristics of the area. However, two caveats should be entered. Firstly, an area already occupied by the middle class is unlikely to be further improved, even though there is likely to be pressure from the residents to designate the area in order to protect their investment.

Secondly, it cannot be assumed that an area without real architectural or historic interest will be gentrified by being designated as a conservation area. There has to be a view among those who might buy or rent property that the area is attractive or interesting in itself.

3.16 The same process can also apply to retail or other commercial premises where the owners or occupiers are willing to pay higher prices or rents for buildings perceived to have some historic, architectural, or cultural merit. This may be true of, say, an old industrial area which becomes occupied by craft workshops, or of an area which is seen as an attractive location by comparison (or 'recreational') shoppers, or of an area which is seen as attractive for certain kinds of offices.

3.17 In effect, the initial public or private investment may not only fill a gap that the market left to itself, following the Davis and Whinston 'neighbourhood effect', would not; it will also give leverage to further private investment, both in upgrading other buildings in the area and in the creation or retention of businesses that would otherwise have failed or left. However, this is only the medium-term effect.

3.18 In this way some commercial areas, and indeed some cities, may change in character as regeneration occurs and their social and commercial character becomes determined by their physical character.

3.19 The argument can be extended to the longer-term process of cumulative upgrading, as the influx of new skills reinforces the local entrepreneurial base and improves the image of the area. Such a process is akin to multiplier analysis, which has been extensively considered in relation to regional development (Richardson 1969) and the role of specific industries such as tourism (Archer et al 1974; Henderson et al 1975). The mechanisms that are supposed to underpin this longer-term cumulative upgrading are the fundamental changes that have taken place in the past 25 years or so in the underlying economic function of cities, in the locational factors that influence both the location and success of new businesses, and in the growing belief in the role of both skills and migrants (see, for example, Keeble 1989) in influencing the rate of new business formation and success.

3.20 To take these arguments individually: cities, it is argued, have ceased to have an important function in the direct production and distribution of goods. Rather they are reverting to the functions that they had before the industrial revolution as sites for administration, business services, and commercial activity, as generators of cultural services, and, increasingly, as the providers of urban amenities, both enhancing the quality of life of their residents and providing the economic base for urban tourism and other leisure-oriented service industries. The key difference, however, to the pre-industrial era is that these activities now contribute a major and growing part of urban economic output and welfare. As a result, the mass of the population, and consequently industrial output and services, are no longer rooted to the countryside by low-productivity agriculture.

3.21 As the physical production and distribution of goods is increasingly decentralised from large cities, other service-type activities are becoming more urban in their choice of location. Meanwhile people are freer that ever before to choose the type of environment in which they live and work. Thus cities which offer a better environment can increasingly attract residents. They in turn contribute their skills to, and spend their incomes with, urban businesses. For these reasons it is argued that traditional factors such as the availability of natural resources or physical infrastructure, and ports or main railway lines, are of declining importance in determining local economic prosperity. Non-traditional factors such as amenities, the quality of the environment, and quality of life are increasingly important. In this view, by contributing to urban amenities and the quality of the urban environment, conservation can significantly assist a city's transition to a new economic role. Those cities that fail to provide a high-quality living environment will increasingly be depleted of highly skilled labour, of entrepreneurial talent, and of new economic activities to replace the old functions that are inevitably being lost.

3.22 The cumulative effect is seen to lie in the degree of self-selection involved. Those who are attracted by the quality of the urban environment will tend to spend their incomes on urban cultural and recreational activities, and, of course, on enhancing their personal investment in houses. There is also evidence that the rate of new and successful business formation tends to be higher among immigrants and the more educated; groups attracted by the enhanced living environment urban conservation can help to generate.

3.23 Although perhaps not stated in exactly this way, these kinds of ideas certainly seem to have influenced urban policy makers. For example, Hall and Cheshire (1987), in summarising the common features of successful urban policy, wrote:

> ... we can see from the successful cases — several in the United States, including some older industrial cities,

some in Europe — that most share some key features. There is a concentrated, simultaneous effort to revitalise a substantial swathe of the inner city most affected by previous decline. This invariably involved redevelopment of part of the downtown for shops and offices, sympathetic conservation and rehabilitation of a nearby waterfront or historic area for leisure activities, comprehensive upgrading of the inner-city housing stock, block by block, associated with architecturally-sympathetic new private housing close by — and improvement of access, especially through improved public transport.

Some of the evidence relating to a number of these urban regeneration initiatives has been analysed by Pearce (1994). The part played in them by successful urban conservation and the adaptation of the specific heritage of the local built environment has yet to be investigated, particularly the role of key factors.

3.24 Although conservation would appear to have a part to play in some successful urban regenerative schemes, it is certainly not a necessary condition for success, since some schemes have not included conservation areas, nor is it a sufficient condition, as some urban conservation areas have not resulted in further urban regeneration. As shown above, economic mechanisms can be elucidated which would suggest how conservation may lead to regeneration. In the examination of any successful regeneration scheme, however, it is difficult to distinguish the variables which have resulted in that success. This is particularly true when public sector authorities have targeted an area and adopted several policies in addition to conservation of the built fabric specifically to assist and encourage regeneration.

3.25 In successful urban regeneration schemes, some key factors, in addition to conservation policy, have been identified. Public funds have been used to improve both the environment and the infrastructure, either directly or through tax incentives. Public/private sector partnerships have sometimes been created to carry through involvement in the area, either generally or through the renovation or development of particular buildings or sites. However, the reporting on these schemes as examples of successful urban regeneration tends to be relatively uncritical, so that it is difficult to distinguish the key economic and policy variables.

Chapter 4 Valuing the urban environment

Introduction

4.1 A number of approaches have been suggested in order to ensure in some way that the best choices are made in decisions concerning the public domain. Purely financial considerations are of little help here, because no charges may be levied and no profits made, but the benefits which accrue to one group of people outweigh the costs which may often be borne by a different group.

4.2 From an economic viewpoint, these benefits and costs can, in principle, be valued, and later chapters will indicate ways in which this may be done. There are, however, problems with this approach if it is intended to be used to guide the process of deciding, before the event, on the best of the alternatives available. Firstly, the cost of finding the right prices and of valuing each alternative will usually be too great to make the process feasible. Secondly, a project which imposes costs on one group and awards benefits to another has redistributional effects which may be politically unacceptable.

4.3 For both these reasons, methods other than Cost-Benefit Analysis have been refined in order to provide cheaper, more useful, alternatives. The closest to Cost-Benefit Analysis is the Planning Balance Sheet Analysis (PBSA). The PBSA, originally put forward in 1956, was explicitly devised to overcome the fact that many social costs and benefits are not easily measured in money terms, so that the results of any social Cost-Benefit Analysis were, and remain, always liable to objections that some costs or benefits have been valued incorrectly. Thus the approach stopped short of assigning values to many costs or benefits, simply indicating where they should be placed on the balance sheet, either as assets or liabilities. Lichfield (1988) developed it into a Community Impact Analysis (CIA) or Community Impact Evaluation (CIE). This method indicated which sections of the community were likely to gain or lose from a planning, or in this case conservation, decision, thus taking the distributional effects into account as well as what might be called the efficiency effects.

4.4 Another type of approach is the multicriteria analysis developed by Nijkamp and others (Nijkamp 1975, 1988; Paelinck 1976; Voogd 1988). Here the various alternatives are ranked according to criteria thought to be relevant; the 'best' is then chosen by calculating the extent to which it outranks others on average. The problem, as Buckley (1988) pointed out in an exchange with Voogd (1988), is that unless the best alternative outweighs the others on all criteria, a weight, explicit or implicit, is being attributed to the attainment of each criterion of each alternative, and this weighting is to some extent subjective.

4.5 An even more mathematical approach to decision-making between alternatives in the absence of full information is the Analytic Hierarchy Process developed by Saaty (1980; and see Zahedi 1986). This has also been suggested for the evaluation of alternative approaches to conservation and restoration by Lombardi and Sirchia (1990) and Roscelli and Zorzi (1990) in Italy. But this too was designed to formalise the process of choosing between alternatives in the absence of full information.

4.6 In the research reported here, the researchers were asked to report on what was known about the value of conservation. The question at issue is not what is probably the best thing to do in the circumstances, but what is known about the results of decisions. This implies an attempt to value the effects of a policy after it has been carried out. In these circumstances, since the desire is to reach generalisable conclusions, it seemed necessary to take a Cost-Benefit Analysis (CBA) approach. This has powerful attractions: it is at least broadly grounded in economic theory and, perhaps even more crucially, it resolves the weighting problem in an objective way. Ultimately the importance (or weight) attached to specific outcomes in the above approaches may be to some extent subjective. By expressing outcomes in money terms and attempting to estimate those values directly or indirectly from people's observed behaviour or stated preferences, CBA derives weights in a systematic way. It is also a technique which makes it much easier to avoid counting the same outcome more than once. It continues to be the favoured framework of analysis as demonstrated by, for example, Greffe (1990), and it would seem to be the most appropriate in the present context.

4.7 Urban conservation involves both costs and benefits. The remit of this study is to analyse ways in which the benefits can be evaluated, but it is nevertheless appropriate at least to summarise the main elements of cost. These fall into two main categories: direct costs and indirect costs. Most costs are almost certainly direct. They are incurred in both the private and public sectors. Individual property owners (including non-public agencies such as the National Trust) undertake expenditures; listing and other regulations impose additional costs on them. Furthermore, public funds are used directly in the conservation of historic buildings, and the administration of conservation consumes real resources. Conservation also has its indirect costs, most obviously the foregone values of redevelopment. The concern here, however, is with the benefits of conservation. In a CBA framework, it is easy to understand why, as discussed at the Cambridge conference, the benefits are to a significant extent indirect, and are therefore not adequately reflected in market prices. It is on the benefits that the discussion now focuses.

4.8 The general problem of how to place a monetary valuation on 'non-traded' goods (those which are not bought and sold in the market place, but from which consumers nonetheless derive positive benefits), has been addressed at length in the literature relating to the natural environment. There are numerous articles addressing the issue of how to value environmental quality or the amount that consumers would be willing to pay to preserve a forest or canal. There is, however, surprisingly little evidence relating to the appraisal of the benefits which consumers derive from the preservation of historic buildings, and much of what does exist is purely anecdotal and not economically rigorous (see, for example, Owen and Hendon 1985). The aim of this section is to outline the main methods which have been developed to place a value on environmental attributes, and which could be applied to the valuation of our built heritage. These methods are:

• Hedonic Pricing

• Travel Cost

• Contingent Valuation

In addition, some reference is made in Appendix 1 to other methods and approaches, such as the Delphi Technique. They can be classified according to whether they seek to place a value on the good or attribute directly, by asking respondents about their willingness to pay for an improvement or to accept a degradation, or indirectly, by using prices from a related market which does exist. Contingent Valuation is an example of the former type, while the Hedonic Pricing and Travel Cost approaches are examples of the latter. Each will be outlined below, together with examples of applications and actual valuations where appropriate. A description of the potential difficulties which may arise with their implementation is given in Appendix 1.

The Hedonic Pricing Method

4.9 The Hedonic Pricing Method (HPM) was developed by Rosen (1974), based on the earlier consumer theory work of Lancaster (1966). It aims to determine the relationship between the attributes of a good and its price, and is arguably the most theoretically rigorous of the valuation methods. Strongly rooted in microeconomic consumer theory, it takes as its starting point the proposition that any differentiated product unit can be viewed as a bundle of characteristics, each with its own implicit — or 'shadow' — price. In the case of housing, for example, the characteristics may be structural, such as the number of bedrooms, size of plot, or presence or absence of a garage, or environmental, such as air quality, the presence of views, noise levels, crime rate, or proximity to shops or schools. Accordingly, the difference between two houses, identical in every respect except that one has

double glazing, should accurately reflect consumers' valuation of the double glazing. Likewise, in the context of the listing of historic buildings or the designation of conservation areas, it is theoretically possible to attribute the impact of such listing or designation by observing the difference in value between two identical buildings, one in a conservation area and the other not. Thus the price of a given property can be viewed as the sum of the shadow prices of its characteristics.

Applications

4.10 A large number of similar hedonic studies considering the effect of environmental and neighbourhood variables on house prices have been undertaken in recent years. With the exception of that by Hough and Kratz (1983), however, there have been very few papers concerned with commercial buildings. Typically, these applications test the effect of proximity to, for example, a forest or Site of Special Scientific Interest (SSSI) on local house prices. Garrod and Willis (1991a) used HPM to explore the impact of the proximity of various types of forest on house prices. They found that the presence of forestry may have a large positive impact. A similar result was observed in the case of location near waterways (Willis and Garrod 1993b). Garrod and Willis (1991b) used HPM to determine the effect of countryside characteristics on surrounding properties. They observe that the presence of a canal or river raises the value of a property by an average of 4.9%, and that the proximity of at least 20% woodland cover raises it by 7.1% above that of an identical property without these features. Maani and Kask (1991) and Pennington et al (1990) estimated house purchasers' Willingness To Pay (WTP) to avoid being close to a high pressure gas pipeline and an aircraft flight path respectively, as reflected in the additional expenditure they were willing to make on a comparable property outside the area. Both find only small WTP to avoid proximity to a negative environmental attribute. Cheshire and Sheppard (1994) used locational as well as structural characteristics in a hedonic price regression study of the price of housing in Reading and Darlington. This allowed for the estimation of how the value of location-specific attributes is capitalised into land prices if they are not included as independent variables. Among the variables included are local amenities provided through the land use planning system.

4.11 There is also a significant body of research into the impact of architectural style and historic zone designation on property valuation. Asabere et al (1989), for example, showed that architectural style has a strong impact on the value of residential property. In their sample of 500 properties sold in Newport, Massachussetts, USA, between 1983 and 1985, older types of architecture commanded significant premiums.Certain styles were particularly valued (Victorian, 20% premium, Garrison, 21% premium, Federal, 20% premium). Moorhouse and

Smith (1994), in their study of nineteenth-century terrace houses in Boston, also found that individuality of any style commands a higher price.

4.12 Hough and Kratz (1983) argued that architecture has certain public good characteristics which may be undervalued in the market. On the basis of a study of office rents, they found that tenants were prepared to pay a premium for new buildings with high values of architectural quality, but not for old buildings of comparable architectural stature. Ford (1989) evaluated the effect of Historic District designation on the prices of properties sold in Baltimore, Maryland, USA, between 1980 and 1984. Designation was found to have a positive but insignificant impact. This result was corroborated by Asabere *et al (op cit)* and also by Shaeffer and Millerick (1991) in their study of the prices of 252 properties in Chicago before and after designation.

The Travel Cost Method

4.13 The Travel Cost Method (TCM) was developed by Clawson and Knetsch (1966). It was based on the premise that the cost of travel to recreational sites can be used as a measure of visitors' willingness to pay. The real costs of travelling to a site were taken as a proxy for the price of the product. Thus, even if visitors did not pay to use a site, they may have incurred expenditure either explicitly or implicitly in travelling to it. This could be used as a measure of (or at least as a lower limit to) their valuation of that site. The explicit costs would be petrol or public transport fares, while the time spent on the visit could be perceived as an implicit cost. Whether on-site and travelling time should be incorporated into the estimate of total cost is a point of debate in the literature. For sites to which the majority of visitors walk, valuing the time they take is the only measure which can feasibly be used (Harrison and Stabler 1981). This might suggest that on-site time should be the true focus of the debate. If it is decided to include on-site or travelling time, it may be difficult to assign a value to it. The opportunity cost in terms of foregone earnings or leisure time which could have been spent doing something else might provide the basis.

Applications
4.14 The volume of studies employing the TCM is considerably smaller than that for the two other main valuation methods. It consists almost exclusively of the estimation of consumer surplus for visits to mainly rural recreational sites such as forests or canals. These applications can be categorised according to whether they use an individual, zonal, or hedonic formulation of the travel cost model, or a combination of all three. Englin and Mendelsohn (1991), for example, estimated the value of alterations in the quality of forest sites using a hedonic travel cost model. They found that certain site attributes, such as 'dirt tracks' and alpine fir trees, had

certain saturation levels, below which they were an economic good, but above which they were a bad. Hanley and Ruffel (1992) used the TCM to evaluate consumer surplus across different types of forestry, each with different physical characteristics. The study showed a strong relationship between visits per year and the mean height of trees, reason for visit, length of stay, and importance of visit. Most forest characteristics were insignificant in the regression, and this was attributed to poor measurement. Willis and Garrod (1991a) compared estimates of consumer surplus for visits to various forest sites using both ITCM and ZTCM. They found that the individual method resulted in considerably smaller consumer surplus estimates, as did Garrod and Willis (1991b). A study of the Lancaster and Montgomery Canals (Willis, Garrod and Dobbs 1990), and another of four botanic gardens (Garrod *et al* 1991), found that consumer surplus valuations were estimated to be significantly lower than the financial operating loss. In the latter study, the average actual valuations of the botanic gardens per trip were found to vary between £1.03 and £11.39 for the four gardens studied. Applications to the valuation of the quality of fishing (Smith *et al* 1991) and deer-hunting sites (Loomis *et al* 1991) have also been considered.

The Contingent Valuation Method

4.15 In contrast with Hedonic Pricing and the Travel Cost Method, which are indirect methods of eliciting valuations from consumers by considering their revealed consumption in related markets which exist, the Contingent Valuation Method (CVM) directly questions consumers on their stated Willingness To Pay for, say, an environmental improvement, or their Willingness To Accept (WTA) compensation for a fall in the quality of the environment. Since respondents are questioned directly, it is possible to ask them whether they would be willing to pay, for example, to preserve a recreational site or even a tropical rain forest of which they are not users. Thus one advantage of the method over others is that it is possible to obtain, at least in principle, option and existence valuations as well as user values.

Applications
4.16 A rapid growth in the number of applications of some form of CVM has taken place in the last decade or so. This may be partly attributed to the potential ability of the method to value option and existence values. The option value of various Sites of Special Scientific Interest (SSSI) was found to be between 10% and 20% of the total site valuation (Willis 1989). Bateman *et al* (1994) established that visitors were willing to pay an average of £22.12 and residents £26.03 per person per year to preserve the existing landscape. In the same study, they also found that consumers were willing to pay an average of approximately £80 per person per year to preserve the Norfolk Broads. Lockwood *et al* (1993) used a CVM

survey in order to assess WTP to preserve national parks in Victoria, Australia. They used a dichotomous choice approach, and estimated the probability of being prepared to pay according to various explanatory variables using a logit regression model. The survey highlighted the relative importance of existence and bequest values, which constituted 35% and 36% of the total valuation respectively. The sample WTP estimate was aggregated to the whole population, adjusting for differences in socio-economic characteristics between the sample average and population, to yield a valuation for the whole population of Victoria of Australian $14m. Non-use value was found to be over three times that of use value in a survey of the Somerset Levels and Moors Environmentally Sensitive Area (ESA) scheme (Garrod *et al* 1994). Other related areas of application of contingent valuation have included improved park facilities (Combs *et al* 1993), a ban on the burning of straw (Hanley 1988), the benefits of canals (Willis and Garrod 1993b), and forestry characteristics (Hanley and Ruffel 1992 and 1993). In the last study, visitors were found to be willing to pay an average of £0.93 per person per visit in the form of an entrance fee.

4.17 In a paper most closely related to the present study, Willis *et al* (1993) assessed the usefulness of the CVM for estimating people's willingness to pay to gain access to Durham Cathedral. They considered CVM to be a 'constant, robust and efficient estimator of WTP', which at approximately £0.80 per person per visit was found to be almost twice the average contribution paid, although since only those actually visiting the cathedral were questioned, non-use value was not measured. The aggregate valuation of the cathedral was around £388,125 per year.

Overview

4.18 A number of possible methods of valuing non-market goods have been examined, and their relative strengths and weaknesses highlighted. Although together HPM, TCM, and CVM account for the vast majority of practical applications, other methods are summarised in Appendix 1.

4.19 Hedonic Pricing embodies the value that consumers place on environmental attributes only in so far as they are capitalised into property prices. Thus the technique is not suitable for considering option, existence or bequest values, nor does it incorporate valuations by visitors.

4.20 Willis, Shafer *et al* (1993) argued that travel cost studies work best when the majority of the visitors live at a large distance from the site. Hence travel cost models may be inadequate for the valuation of urban recreational sites, where the distance travelled is likely to be smaller than that which would ideally be required by the technique. It appears, then, that the Travel Cost Method is perhaps the least preferred of the three, since it has neither the strong economic theoretical underpinning and well developed econometric theory of Hedonic Pricing, nor the potential to measure wider non-use values of Contingent Valuation.

4.21 Contingent Valuation is possibly the least rigorous, but arguably now the most popular, of the three main valuation techniques. It has become widely accepted by politicians, since it is compatible with the concept of democracy and valuation by the population at large.

Chapter 5 Literature review of cases

Introduction

5.1 In the UK and other countries included in this study, details of property transactions, including investment in conservation projects, are not generally published. This is disappointing, since the conservation of the built environment in its widest sense undoubtedly involves substantial investment by property owners and third parties such as public agencies. It is not possible to estimate accurately the full extent of investment in conservation in the UK, but it covers a wide range of activities involving houses, town centres, churches, commercial properties, and what are described as heritage properties, including castles and other historic buildings. Investment may be small in comparison to the general level of property investment but, as an example, English Heritage offered grants totalling £50.7 million relating to 3804 projects in 1993–4.

5.2 The absence of well researched and carefully analysed case studies is also disappointing, since investment in conservation often has broader objectives than the simple economic return. Urban regeneration and town centre renewal often involve investment in conservation in order to provide a framework for increased activity and investment. This is often described as 'pump priming', and there is much anecdotal evidence that conservation has been successful in this regard.

5.3 In order to give a broader picture than that provided by the literature review, a study has been made of the cases which have been published or publicised. (These are included in Appendix 2.) It should, however, be noted that these cases are often used as marketing material or publicity, and do not necessarily form an accurate and balanced report. It is also likely that much of the published material relates to the most successful cases, while those instances which did not achieve their objectives go unreported.

5.4 The cases that are included in this report and its appendices do not represent a balanced position, but they do provide useful material and the basis for further research.

5.5 The economic performance of individual properties in the UK is almost always regarded as a confidential matter. This discourages case-by-case analysis and research. From the information available, it is clear that conservation property is affected by normal economic circumstances. Its success, both financially and in its broader objectives, is largely dependent on local economic circumstances such as supply and demand. The case studies do, however, provide a basis for investigating whether investment in conservation can enhance the economic and social performance of an area. In some cases, it may be a means of arresting decline, in others (for example in the Old Town of Edinburgh) the best method for implementing urban renewal strategies and encouraging tourism.

5.6 One factor that has become clear during this study is that the publications appear to be growing both in number and usefulness. This may be due in part to a recognition of the difficulties caused by structural changes in the established property-holding bodies such as the Ministry of Defence, the Health Service, and transport companies. The publication of case studies on the conversion of military sites (Wiltshire County Council *et al* 1995) and the creation of organisations such as the Railway Heritage Trust are examples.

The selection of reported cases

5.7 The thinnest and outermost layer of our comprehension of the value of conservation is that of journalistic and public relations hyperbole, fostered by both its proponents and its critics. Beneath this layer, however, there is a wide range of empirical assessments carried out by local authorities, government agencies, property owners, consultants, and academics. These case studies provide an insight into the development of research on conservation, as well as helping to understand how the conservation of the cultural built heritage works. This chapter draws on a selection of these case studies to provide four contrasting scenarios illustrating the ways in which conservation of the built environment works. It also suggests how future research on the evaluation of the dynamic externalities of the conservation of the cultural built heritage may be addressed.

5.8 Documented case studies were located by four principal means. In early December 1994 a letter was sent to ten Urban Development Corporations (UDCs) in England, requesting information on research which they had either undertaken or commissioned on the socio-economic impact of conservation in their areas. Interviews with senior officials from those UDCs in which conservation had been an important element in urban regeneration revealed that detailed evaluations had not been undertaken. However, these interviews did suggest that structured discussions with key individuals were themselves a valuable means of understanding how conservation works. This view is supported both by the earlier research undertaken by the University of Cambridge, and by the recently introduced methodology for evaluating the effectiveness of the UDCs (Headicar 1994 and PIEDA/DoE 1995).

5.9 A second means of collecting case studies was to request information from a select number of local authorities. This produced few responses, confirming the difficulty of locating data even at a local level, and an apparent underestimation of the financial significance of planning and conservation issues. Many authorities regard committee papers which may provide useful information as private documents not normally available for publication because they contain financial information which is usually discussed in closed session. This is regrettable; the usefulness of this source of information is demonstrated by material supplied by North Devon District Council in relation to Ilfracombe, and by East Lindsay District Council. Some councils attach such an importance to conservation that it forms a major part of their economic development activities. Examples include Bath City Council, Canterbury City Council, and Cotswold District Council.

5.10 The third source was academic and professional publications in Britain and (to a limited extent) France, which increasingly include reports on conservation projects. The range of articles is wide, and the method of reporting varies considerably. The publications cover the disciplines of planning, geography, and architecture; examples include *Conservation Today.* They provide an indication of the range of projects which could be the subject of detailed assessment. (Other examples include Legal and General 1995, Calthorpe Estate 1995, and Marcus 1995.)

5.11 Following the seminar held in London in June 1995, a further request was made for case study material, which produced a substantial amount of material covering a wide range of projects, summarised in Appendix 2. This shows a wide range of sources of material, many of which could form the basis of further analysis. They still, however, represent an unbalanced picture of conservation in the UK, and only two of the cases relate to Europe.

The value of case studies

5.12 Throughout Europe and North America, a variety of policy mechanisms have been instrumental in securing the conservation of the cultural built heritage. The majority have not been directed exclusively towards this objective. The review of case studies, therefore, was not confined to the externalities arising from conservation policies as exercised in particular countries (assuming that these could be isolated in the first place). Rather it concentrated on research into externalities arising in areas where building conservation and environmental enhancement have been achieved.

5.13 The selection of case studies in this manner finds support from the Council of Europe, which notes that:

The notion of 'conservation' transcends the division of buildings which are legally 'protected' and those which are not, embracing both groups. It refers not only to the cost of actual upkeep and restoration work but also to expenses for running, management and re-use where applicable. (Council of Europe 1991, *Funding the architectural heritage.*)

5.14 The cases assembled in this study include some from property owners who object to the impact of conservation controls on the management of their property (Legal and General 1995 and Calthorpe Estate 1995). In general the cases are supportive of conservation, but they lack detail. It appears that worthwhile quantitative material can be obtained on a consistent basis only when there is an obligation to provide it. Without this, the limited amount of material available demonstrates the usefulness of an understanding of the economic and social value of conservation, particularly since demands on conservation funding are growing as increasing numbers of conservation areas are created and the number of protected buildings increases. The studies demonstrate that without public funding many conservation projects could not proceed (Ripon Borough Council 1995, Ilfracombe Civic Trust 1992, Brigg Civic Trust 1992, and Edinburgh City Council 1995).

5.15 The case studies do not include the impact of lottery funding in the UK, and no studies have been found to relate to lottery funding for the heritage elsewhere. An increase in the number of financial appraisals in support of lottery funding bids can be expected, and these might provide useful data, particularly if they can be linked to case studies and project reviews.

Synthesis of case studies

5.16 The conclusions to be drawn from the review of case studies must remain general for two reasons:

- firstly, although the review does not claim to be comprehensive, it indicates that the socio-economic externalities of the conservation of the cultural built heritage are seldom examined in any degree of detail. The conclusions, therefore, are blunted by the inadequacies of research across a range of locations.

- secondly, and relatedly, the review suggested that 'conservation' is an imprecise term, which cannot be subjected to rigorous analysis. This is partly due to the fact that the term can be applied to a number of different processes, including the repair, maintenance, and enhancement of:

- the interior of buildings

- the exterior of buildings

- the surrounding environment

Furthermore, rigorous analysis of conservation is made difficult by the fact that it operates on a variety of scales, and can be concentrated or scattered, or spread over differing timescales and periods, with correspondingly varied effects.

5.17 Collectively, however, the case studies illustrate the ways in which conservation works, and point to four potentially contrasting scenarios:

Scenario one: investment in the repair, maintenance, and enhancement of the cultural built heritage utilises materials and labour from the local construction industry and its suppliers. In areas of high unemployment, this is an unquestionable benefit (although that benefit may not come to rest in the area of conservation itself). The numbers of jobs created are increased when other jobs generated indirectly by this expenditure are taken into account (Edinburgh Old Town 1995).

In Finland, the Ministry of the Environment considers the issue to be sufficiently important to have commissioned a study in order to find out the difference between the impact on employment of renovation and modernisation work, and of new construction. This study is being carried out by the Construction Economics Institute of Tampere University of Technology (Salokangas 1995). In the Calderdale Inheritance Project, the consultants estimated that physical works undertaken helped to sustain around 300 person years of construction employment (York Consultancy Ltd and Centre for Urban Development and Environmental Management 1993).

Scenario two: the revitalisation of the cultural built heritage brings a mix of costs and benefits to remaining residents and business occupiers. On the positive side, they benefit from improved conditions, in terms of housing stock and business premises, physical environment, and the upgrading in the quality of locally sold goods and services. Owner-occupiers can also realise substantial equity increases on their properties (provided, of course, that they do not sell them during the early stage of revitalisation). On the other hand, remaining residents/occupiers are likely to meet increased costs: increased rents and rates, high prices of locally sold goods and services, and the loss of previous social, business, and institutional contacts.

Although a number of the case studies recorded increases in property prices (Scribner 1976; Rackham 1977), the majority suggested that increases had occurred but noted that hard evidence was not available. The unavailability of evidence was also noted by the University of Cambridge in its earlier research. The issue is of considerable importance, and is returned to below when considering sources of information for evaluation studies.

Related to the issue of increases in property prices is that of the displacement of low-income and elderly households from revitalised neighbourhoods. Existing research provides only a few insights into this issue (Gale 1991), not least because of the difficulties involved in contacting displaced tenants to interview them about their reasons for moving. Rising costs, as well as pressure from landlords and property agents keen to realise increased capital values, may force some of the original occupiers to move. This, however, is part of a wider social movement in which the poor are displaced by wealthier residents. Rather than perceiving displacement in relation to 'conservation' (which itself refers to a multiciplicity of processes) as a special and somewhat unusual process, it should be understood as one example of the way social and economic change is imprinted on the built environment (Smith and Williams 1987).

The change in use of buildings and/or their intensity of use, and corresponding reductions in vacancy levels and increases in conversions of houses to apartments, have been commented on by a number of authors (De Klerk and Vijgen 1994, Punter 1991, Smith 1984, and Van Duren 1993). An overview of the literature, however, does not enable a firm link to be drawn between these processes and conservation; this is mainly due to a lack of empirical rigour, which is in turn partly the result of the inadequacy of the data sources. The existing studies also largely ignore the key determinants of the property market, including the availability of finance capital and real interest rates (Bougarel 1992 and Legal and General 1995). A valuable source of information in setting this wider context is provided by regular reports published by property advisers (Ambrose 1994).

Scenario three: conservation is an important means by which people maintain their socio-cultural identity; familiar objects indicating shared cultural values are more important than unfamiliar or foreign objects in creating a sense of place (see Ilfracombe 1992 and Hubbard 1993). Furthermore, the repair of vulnerable building elements such as chimney stacks, roofs, copings, parapets and cornices, the cleaning of stonework, the painting of joinery, and improvements to basement areas and railings — all widespread in conservation projects — make an impact on the environment. This can in turn alter people's perception of an area, and influence its ability to attract wealthier residents and higher quality services, as in the previous scenario. Alternatively, if prices increase, private investors may be attracted to buy or improve properties. These effects may in time spread to nearby areas, although the scale of the original work needs to be substantial (Donnison and Middleton 1987; Ripon 1995).

Scenario four: the cultural built heritage takes a decisive share in the dispersed economic flows resulting from tourism (Colardelle 1992), although these are hard to capture (Smith 1984, Patin 1988, Hanna and Binney 1978, and City of Canterbury Planning Department 1975). Investment in conservation enhances the value of a property and makes it more attractive for the visitor, either as the object of a visit or as the backdrop to other leisure activities. Over the last 20 years, the tourist industry has become a key factor in economic development, both nationally and especially locally. Although the market for both domestic and overseas tourists is anticipated to become increasingly competitive by the turn of the century, heritage is widely believed to be a growth area for tourism (Touche Ross 1994). This scenario is likely to grow in importance in the UK as submissions are made to the lottery fund distribution bodies. As a result, an understanding of the economic and social benefits of conservation practice, at least in those cases eligible for lottery funding submission, can be expected to grow.

Tools of evaluation

5.18 It is not possible to trace and measure all of the effects outlined above, but it is clear that in broad terms conservation is effective, if expensive (Williams 1980 and PIEDA/DoE 1995). The comments which follow are designed to help those undertaking research which aims to relate and evaluate the impact of conservation, and provide the information required to monitor these processes in Britain.

5.19 When conservation takes place, it is bound to be reflected to some extent in the economic indicators of the locality. In order to assess its impact it is therefore essential to establish both the current health of the locality and change over time. (The assessment of current conditions is particularly important when attempting to draw comparisons between different areas.) This can be done with reference to a range of socio-economic indicators:

• *property prices/valuations* One key measure of the economic health of an area is the trend in property prices. An area in which property maintains its value (in constant prices or in relation to similar areas) is healthy; demand is sufficient for the area to function well in the overall property market. Information on valuations is, however, fiercely guarded. Property owners would therefore have to be offered an incentive to release the required information. One such incentive would be to link conservation grants to guarantees of periodic property valuations. In the case of house prices, data on sales is available from the Nationwide and Halifax building societies. This information reflects only those houses which come onto the market during the period under examination, however. Because the price movements of this subset may not be typical of the stock as a whole, it is also necessary to obtain some local knowledge of the types and numbers of properties available in the local market in order to make sense of the relative movement in prices. This information can be requested from local residential estate agents.

Since the introduction of the Uniform Business Rate, commercial and residential properties in England and Wales have been valued once every five years. The last valuation was conducted in 1993, providing a useful benchmark for conservation studies due to commence in the short term. Under current legislation, however, access to this information is restricted to rating purposes only.

A detailed examination of the impact of conservation on property prices is therefore permissible only by government.

• *rent* is a function of the quality of the unit in question, the ability of the tenant to pay, and the strength of the rental market. Higher rents for units in one area, relative to those of comparable size in another, thus indicate that the units are of better quality, and/or that the property market is improving in that area. If rents increase more rapidly in one area than in another, it is more likely that investment in the stock of property is occurring in the first area. Because rental data on individual properties is usually treated as confidential, a means of securing access similar to that outlined in relation to valuations would have to be used. The deregulation of the private rented housing market consequent upon the passing of the Housing Act of 1988 allows the impact of conservation on the level of rents for such properties to be assessed. However, the prices quoted in press advertisements are negotiable by 5%, and may be unrepresentative of the stock of rented residential properties within an area. For this reason, data collected from advertised lettings should be supplemented by interviews with local letting agents.

• *vacancy rates* indicate the overall level of demand for an area. A decrease in vacancy rates may indicate a number of things. Fewer vacancies may reflect an absolute increase in population in the area. Usually, however, absolute population increase is not the main reason for a reduction in vacancy rates; a decrease in vacancies more often reflects an improvement in the desirability of an area. Local authorities hold data on vacant properties, but because the information is collected in order to assess rates charges, it cannot be made available to the public without amendment to current legislation.

• *development appraisals* Following the publication of PPG 16, developers and property owners who seek listed building consent are increasingly demonstrating the financial implications of their proposals. Few case studies are available, but a method of appraisal is already emerging in which developers set out the costs and economic viability of proposals, or a range of possible schemes with differing conservation impacts. Such studies give the opportunity to assess the financial and physical benefits and costs of schemes.

• *crime rates* Evidence of crime from the British Crime Survey can be used to measure the real or perceived safety of an area. The use of crime rates as a socio-economic indicator has been criticised on the grounds that it may reflect the relative efficiency of different police forces at convicting criminals, rather than the actual occurrence of crimes. Furthermore, although the desirability of a residential or business location appears to be significantly affected by its crime rates, it is important to remember that crime rates can be used as a two-way indicator, which requires that the results be interpreted with caution.

• *tourism statistics* The ability of an area to attract external leisure-related custom can be measured using statistics on tourism, which can be collected with the assistance of the private sector. The data should cover:

• numbers and source of visitors

• average spend of visitor by category

• day/stay ratios

• accommodation profile of staying visitors

• purpose of visit

• demographic and socio-economic profiles

• other specific topical issues

This information will be important both in terms of informing a wide range of related issues (including the timing and extent of capital investment in tourism, and the management requirements of buildings and areas receiving growing numbers of tourists) and in order to counter threats posed to heritage tourism by other forms of tourism such as shopping tourism. The extent to which the private sector uses the information will depend on whether they can be successfully involved in the setting-up process. The leisure industry is typically unused to having high-quality market research to rely on. However, with a consistent research methodology it will only be a matter of time before the better operators learn to use, and indeed rely on, the information provided.

The growth of tourism is substantial in the UK. A survey conducted by the English Tourist Board reported that two-thirds of all overseas visitors came to the UK because of its heritage. They appear to have taken a broad view of the heritage, ranging from Buckingham Palace to Stonehenge, and from the Tower of London to the streets of Bath. It is possible to identify an increase in shop rental values and hotel rates in those locations that benefit from heritage-linked tourism. This issue of the value of heritage is of increasing interest, particularly in Cost-Benefit Analysis studies, including those of road schemes (Silberson 1994).

• *unemployment rates* Although unemployment has long been used as a key indicator of economic conditions, it is subject to two principal limitations: the frequent changes in the definition of what constitutes unemployment and the difficulty of deriving an appropriate denominator to calculate rates from the raw figures of unemployment totals. In order to overcome the latter limitation, researchers using monthly data collected by the former Department of Employment have adopted two approaches. The first is to use the ratio of long-term unemployment (>1 year) to unemployment in general. The second is to use the estimated numbers of males aged 20–65 and females aged 20–60 as the denominator in order to calculate the rates of unemployment. But since conservation areas are generally small, unemployment rates are of limited use with specific regard to the areas themselves, although they may help in the measurement of more dispersed benefits.

• *employment* The biennial Census of Employment undertaken by the former Department of Employment provides an indication of overall employment and net change in different industries (including construction and repair of buildings). Because the indicator is workplace-based, it fails to distinguish whether the people who get jobs live in the area of conservation or come from elsewhere. It is nevertheless a useful indicator of the number of jobs generated by conservation.

• *population age structure* The socio-economic health of an area is also indicated by the age structure of its population. A high percentage of elderly people may be synonymous with neighbourhood decline. Assuming that elderly homeowners are of low or moderate income and are therefore less able to provide 'sweat equity', their housing may deteriorate faster than that of younger households. The 25–34 age group has relatively high residential mobility. If an area becomes more attractive as a residential location, it should therefore demonstrate this by capturing or retaining a significant proportion of this age cohort. The decennial Census of Population provides a good database. However, this can only be applied to comparable census information from 1991 and 2001 (plans for a 1996 census were cancelled), using the same ward or enumeration district boundaries. Data on the age structure of the population should not be used in isolation, but combined with other socio-economic indicators, also available from the decennial census.

5.20 While each of the socio-economic indicators outlined above is valid for assessing the impact of conservation, their appropriateness will be determined by the objectives of conservation in any one area. These need to be clearly defined at the outset of the evaluation programme, so that the research can be clearly focused. Defining the objectives of the research will also help to ensure that its approach is cognitive and operational, as opposed to descriptive (Coccossis and Nijkamp 1995). Under these conditions, the act of evaluation can play a part in the evolution of conservation, instead of closing the process as in much of the earlier research.

5.21 Much of the debate on evaluation methodologies centres around the use of quantitative versus qualitative indicators. The general consensus is that both have a role to play, and that qualitative/attitudinal indicators are useful in interpreting the reasons for change in socio-economic indicators (Spilsbury 1992). Attitudinal information is relatively expensive to obtain, and available only through surveys of local residents, businesses, and selected stakeholders. Used in conjunction with the quantitative socio-economic indicators, however, it can provide an effective means of developing a general interpretation of the impacts of conservation 'in the round'.

5.22 While evaluative studies will be of assistance in assessing the value of conservation across a range of locations, their conclusions will remain questionable if the wider determinants of the market are ignored. Set within this context, further empirical research should help to guide the evolution of conservation over the years ahead.

5.23 The lack of case-by-case analysis may at first sight appear both astonishing and disappointing, particularly since conservation often involves significant public investment. This difficulty could be overcome if the recipients of public funding were obliged to provide an assessment of the anticipated economic and social benefits or costs at the beginning of the approval process (PIEDA/DoE 1995). This analysis could be revisited when the project is completed. In some cases, where significant information may be provided, a further case review could be undertaken at an appropriate time after the project has 'bedded down'. In this way, a library or database could be created which might provide sufficient resources for a clear and authoritative analysis which would be understood by the market, by investors, and by the occupiers of the properties.

Chapter 6 The implications for valuing urban conservation: conclusions and issues for research

Introduction

6.1 The benefits of conservation have already been identified in principle in Chapter 3 of this report. Methodologies developed almost exclusively in the context of the natural environment have been reviewed in Chapter 4, as has the very limited research which adapts those methodologies to the urban context. In Chapter 5 a sample of case studies was reviewed. The purpose of this final chapter is to try to synthesise earlier research, and to consider how it can be applied in the context of urban conservation.

Static benefits

6.2 The Travel Cost (TCM) and Hedonic Pricing (HPM) methods capture only user benefits. HPM has attractions because of its rigour: it is firmly based in economic theory, and increasingly sophisticated econometric techniques can be used to estimate hedonic prices. HPM is also at an advantage in urban contexts, where a significant proportion of those who value heritage choose to live in or near it. This is the group whose willingness to pay (WTP) is excluded, or very heavily undervalued, using the TCM method. This objection to the TCM method has less force in the context of estimating values for rural recreational sites (such as, say, the New Forest), and even less in the context of the natural environment. This is because of the obvious but significant fact that there are few houses in the vicinity of remote or free-standing environmental attractions, while the opposite is true in the urban context. Indeed the issue is more precisely identifiable than that. The more the benefits of an urban conservation site appeal to residents, the more they will be reflected in the prices of houses, and perhaps also of commercial properties. In principle, therefore, HPM techniques will be more appropriate in estimating those benefits.

6.3 The quality of HPM studies has been very variable; some have been little more than unreflecting exercises in data collection. The methodology has systematically improved, however, and certain general lessons have been learned. It is always essential to have as fully specified a model as possible, and to avoid the obvious econometric problems, but in an urban context it is also essential to include separately the basic value of land purely as space, and the additional price paid for location with respect to centres of employment.

6.4 Both TCM and HPM methods depend on strong assumptions, although those of HPM are less ambitious. While HPM captures the user demand only of residents in and close to the conserved building or area, TCM captures only the user demand of visitors. TCM is therefore more appropriate in the context of 'free-standing' attractions such as Stonehenge, but totally inappropriate for residential or combined residential and heritage areas such as Bath. This suggests an issue for research: in an urban context, how far are the two groups of users (residents and visitors) mutually exclusive? In as much as they are, the WTP of the two groups would effectively be additive. In valuing the user benefits of, say, Bath, the values from both HPM and TCM studies should therefore be added together. Such a procedure would be less valid in York, however, and still less so in Durham or Salisbury; while in Bedford Park, Chiswick, the HPM value would effectively capture all user value. The reason for this suggestion is that people who place a high value on heritage architecture are drawn to live and work in a city such as Bath, both by the quality of the housing and because of the benefits associated with the cityscape and public buildings. Visitors, whose travel costs reflect their WTP for both the residential and public buildings, are also drawn to Bath. So both sets of user values need to be estimated and added together. In the context of the other towns, the expectation is that a progressively smaller proportion of the resident population choose to live in the particular city because of its architectural qualities; and in the case of what is primarily a residential neighbourhood, such as Bedford Park, the number of visitors is insignificant relative to the values placed on its conservation by residents. The findings of Bateman *et al* (1994) should also be noted in this context. Using Contingent Valuation Methods, they found that residents placed a higher value per capita on landscape than did visitors. It would be reasonable to conclude that, by analogy, those who have chosen to live in conservation areas tend to value urban conservation more highly than do those who visit conserved areas. Further light is shed on this issue by an English Heritage study of the attitudes of local residents, compared to those of visitors, to a proposal to reinstate the historical landscape at Kenwood. Visitors were much more favourable to the idea than residents, suggesting that residents specifically valued the local environment near which they had chosen to live.

Conclusion

6.5 In the context of urban conservation, HPM is preferable to TCM, but captures only a variable fraction of user benefits; however, informed judgement indicates approximately how that proportion will vary in different contexts (see above). TCM is not very rigorous, and is usually less applicable in an urban context because of the need to assume that those who value the attraction do not choose to live close to it.

6.6 Contingent Valuation Methods (CVM) have the considerable attraction of potentially capturing all static benefits: that is, user values + existence + option values. The method is not wholly rigorous, but there has been a rapid and recent increase in the number of studies, and techniques have improved very considerably. When the techniques were first suggested, there was voluminous research on theoretical objections such as the free-rider problem, but experimental research (Bohm 1972) suggests that free-riding is not much of a problem in practice. In addition, techniques have been developed which offset the kinds of problems theoreticians have spotlighted. One useful issue for research would be further benchmarking studies of specific contexts where it is possible to compare HPM and CVM values. The few examples of such studies (all in the context of the natural environment) suggest that, in addition to providing a measure of non-user values, estimates from CVM can be reasonably consistent with those from other methods where they are comparably identified. But not enough comparative studies have been done in any context to allow safe conclusions to be drawn, and none at all have been done in an urban context.

6.7 In an urban context, systematic CVM research (cross-checked against HPM and TCM estimates where appropriate) would be the most useful. CVM techniques could be applied equally in a wide range of contexts, from individual buildings and heritage sites to whole areas. The only such study that has been identified (as compared to numerous hypothetical examples in, for example, Greffe 1990) is that by Willis *et al* (1993) of Durham Cathedral. The authors included only visitors, and calculated a total value of £388,125 per annum: to this should be added the value to residents, which in Durham is unlikely to be very large. If it is taken to be perhaps 20% of the value ascribed to visitors, that would yield a total of £465,750. Studies by the same authors and by others have typically found that, in the context of the natural environment, non-user values account for between 35% and 75% of the total value. If, in the case of Durham, this was conservatively placed at 40%, then the total static benefits associated with Durham Cathedral would be £652,050 per annum rather than the £388,125 that relates to visitors alone.

6.8 An unanswered issue identified in the review of case studies was that raised by Hubbard (1993): to what extent do people derive a sense of place from and attach value to a general townscape, as opposed to individual buildings or groups of buildings? This is clearly an issue for research, since the answer would have implications for the form of urban conservation. For example, does conserving only the outward appearance of buildings, or even just their facades, in most cases produce benefits as or nearly as great (at least in economic terms) as conserving those buildings in their historic integrity ? However, it is necessary to bear in mind that historic buildings are primary sources of evidence about the past. The

information they provide is not available from any other source. The buildings are primary documents, the equivalent of archives, and so have an academic value. Their potential to sustain future research and understanding is largely destroyed if they are reduced to shells, even though their contribution to the character of the place in which they stand might not be significantly diminished (though in such cases it often is).

6.9 For measuring the static benefits derived from urban conservation, then, the most promising method would seem to be CVM, but there are still virtually no applications of the method to valuing examples of urban (as opposed to natural) environmental values. More studies are urgently needed of a range of types of conservation along the lines suggested in paragraph 6.4.

Dynamic benefits

6.10 It can be seen how markets fail to reflect the potential benefits of urban conservation fully, or even at all. In addition to the problems of market failure identified in Chapter 1, dynamic benefits are subject to a high degree of risk and uncertainty. This is itself an argument, on the insurance principle, for public funding. The risks and uncertainties should be spread over the widest possible group, so there is a case for arguing that they should be borne, at least in part, by local or national government.

6.11 A further implication of this was raised in the review of property market attitudes to the benefits of conservation. Is there a 'long-term' versus a 'short-term' view? It could be the case, for example, that historic estates are simply taking a longer-term view of the impact of conservation on income flows than is typically taken by commercial developers. In the long term, in addition, it may be possible for owners to 'capture' (or internalise) more of the benefits . This suggests a possible issue for research: what precisely accounts for the differences in attitudes to urban conservation of owners of historic estates compared to commercial developers? If it could be explained in terms of differing time horizons, this might influence commercial developers to be more sympathetic to conservation.

6.12 It would not be helpful to suggest values for urban conservation or regeneration at this stage, because there is simply no concrete information. The reasons for this are obvious once the problem is specified. The total value generated by urban regeneration would be approximately the GDP of the area, minus that part of it which represents GDP diverted from other areas. Part of this net increase in value would be the result of expenditure on conservation, non-financial conservation measures such as designation of a conservation area, and the increase in certainty resulting from such measures. But it is not possible even to measure the net increase in

GDP associated with urban regeneration, let alone identify, in a quantitative sense, the part played in it by urban conservation.

6.13 That does not mean that nothing useful can be said or done. Given the problems of precise estimation, the most useful approach would be to have detailed and objective case studies, including cases where conservation spending has not been conspicuously successful in economic as well as heritage terms, such as in Liverpool (a possible issue for research). A number of case studies were reviewed in Chapter 4, but none of these was done with the explicit view of exploring the benefits of conservation. Nor were they done within an economic framework, such as Cost-Benefit Analysis, which conceptually clarifies the nature of the benefits of conservation, avoids double counting, and separates distributional effects from potential gains in welfare. Case studies directed to illuminating the nature, sources, and potential scale of the benefits of urban conservation, as well as its distributional effects, should be informed by the appropriate definition of the problem as identified above.

6.14 The behaviour of agencies charged with urban (or even local) regeneration reveals a common judgement that urban conservation plays an important role in a wider strategy for the improvement of the urban environment. Thus in continental Europe, Britain, and the USA successful urban regeneration is typically the result of a coordinated strategy involving:

• the conservation and restoration of historic buildings or districts

• traffic calming and pedestrianisation

• the provision of attractive owner-occupied housing (often in converted historic buildings)

• a range of other actions including upgrading infrastructure, investment in training and education, and help for small businesses

Perhaps the best known cases in Britain at the urban scale would include Glasgow and Norwich. There are also more localised instances, for example in the jewellery quarter of Birmingham or Covent Garden in London. One of the earliest examples in Europe at an urban scale was provided by Bologna, but there are also examples in France such as Rouen or Lille, or in Spain, notably Barcelona. Despite the publicity conservation has had as an instrument of urban regeneration in the USA, the examples there tend to be more localised: for example the port area in Baltimore, Ghirredeli Square in San Francisco, the old tram shed in Salt Lake City, or the old train station in St Louis. While it is easy to list these examples (as in Greffe 1990 or Pearce 1994), it is much more difficult to identify the specific role played by urban conservation.

6.15 These examples suggest a number of issues for research. Apart from the need to identify more precisely the contribution of urban conservation to urban regeneration, there are also specific questions:

• what, if any, role is played by 'anchor' buildings?

• what contribution to entrepreneurship can restored residential, commercial, and industrial areas play?

• what is the minimum scale of effective action? This was considered from the viewpoint of urban tourism in Ashworth and Tunbridge 1990, but the review of the planning case studies suggested that this is perhaps a more complex issue. It is not just a question of the number of buildings, or the area that is conserved (Smith 1984), but also of the critical mass of people whose lives and lifestyles are potentially altered (De Klerk and Vijgen 1984).

• what scale of conservation is required to generate a potential for the development of satisfying urban lifestyles which, in turn, reinforces the success of the initial conservation effort by attracting new residents and businesses to serve those residents?

• is the mix of buildings critical in this process?

• what role does the image of a city play in its regeneration, and how can conservation contribute to that image?

• what is the most effective administrative structure?

• what is the most effective funding mechanism?

• how much private investment does a given expenditure of public funds generate?

• are there factors which influence in a systematic way the leveraging effect of public funds?

6.16 In Chapter 5 it was found that information available was not sufficient to allow one to conclude whether, to what extent, and in what circumstances conservation could have favourable dynamic impacts on property prices. This is true in England and Wales. In Scotland, however, the Register of Sassines might in principle allow these questions to be addressed systematically . An issue for research, therefore, might be to trace the movement of relative values in matched areas. This should be done over an extended period in order to cancel out as far as possible the fluctuations caused by general, macroeconomically determined price cycles. Some of these areas would be selected because they had not been significantly influenced by conservation, others because they had. It would obviously be important, although difficult, to choose areas with architectural and socio-economic characteristics that matched as closely as possible.

6.17 Case studies could also throw light on another issue for research, the dynamic displacement and redistributional effects of urban conservation. Even though these are not strictly benefits or costs, they are socially relevant, and influence people's perceptions of conservation.

6.18 A final, and perhaps the most obvious, issue for research is to identify precisely what information requirements should be imposed on the recipients of conservation-related grants. This report has highlighted both a dearth of studies on the benefits of urban conservation and a general lack of systematic data. Yet grants for conservation purposes are made, and it would be comparatively easy to identify information which the recipients of these grants should provide in order to derive a more precise evaluation of both the static and the dynamic benefits of conservation, and to monitor systemically the impact of conservation. The review that we have undertaken provides clear indications of the kind of information that is needed, but collecting and analysing information costs resources. There is no point in imposing greater costs of information collection on grant recipients than are strictly necessary. An issue for research, therefore, is exactly what information could be

collected in the most cost-efficient way, and perhaps whether there should be more general requirements of collaboration with more detailed specific studies that might be commissioned by conservation bodies from time to time.

Conclusion

6.19 There is no present answer, in a numeric sense, to the question, 'what are the dynamic benefits of urban conservation?' It is certain, though, that they can be large and positive, although this is not the case in all circumstances. The best way to address the question would appear to be through detailed and structured case studies, since data do not and, in sufficient quantity, could not exist for econometric studies. Such case studies should be informed by an understanding of how the economic benefits should be defined; they should include examples of unsuccessful as well as of successful cases; and they should attempt not only to identify the overall contribution of conservation, but also to examine more specific questions, including those listed above. In addition, the awarding of conservation-related grants should be made conditional on the provision of data, which would be used, in confidence, to evaluate the benefits of conservation.

Appendix 1 Valuation of social costs and benefits: methodologies

The Hedonic Pricing Method

After deciding which environmental attribute is of most interest to the study, the HPM consists of two main steps: calculation of a hedonic equation, followed by estimation of a bid curve for the environmental amenity. The first step is to regress the price of the property (denoted P_h) on all characteristics, both structural (denoted S_i) and environmental (E_j), which are considered relevant to the dependent variable. Thus the relationship

$$P_h = f(S_i, E_j), \quad i=1, ..., v; \, j=1, ..., w.$$

(A1.1)

is estimated if there are v structural and w environmental characteristics in the equation. The shadow price of a given attribute is obtained by differentiating the function (A1.1) partially with respect to that attribute.

The issue of the functional form of, and estimation method for, (A1.1) must be addressed. The function will only be linear in unlikely special cases where additional units of the characteristics are valued equally, for example, if a fifth bedroom is valued as highly as the fourth. Otherwise the equation will be nonlinear. A number of different types of function are possible and have been estimated in the literature, including linear, log-linear, double-log, power transformations, and Box-Cox transformations (Halvorsen and Pollakowski 1981; Cropper et al 1988; Bloomquist and Worley 1981). Ordinary least squares (OLS) was the estimation method traditionally used, but the method of maximum likelihood is becoming increasingly common.

The second step is to estimate a demand curve for the environmental attribute of interest (denoted E_k). If one assumes that the supply of houses with the given attribute is fixed (this is most likely to be the case when one is considering the short run), the implicit demand curve for E_k can be derived by regressing the shadow price of E_k (denoted r), obtained from the first step, on E_k as well as on relevant socio-economic variables such as incomes (Y), ages (A), and variables representing tastes and preferences (T) for a given area I:

$$r_k = g(E_k, Y_k, A_k, T_k)$$

(A1.2)

Total valuations for the attribute can be derived by the summation of the implicit prices across all areas k of interest.

Problems with the Hedonic Pricing Method

There are a number of problems with the use of HPM as a technique for the valuation of non-market goods and, in the present context, of conservation. These have been described in the literature. First, Hedonic Price Models can, by definition, only measure those aspects of value which are embodied into the prices of conserved or surrounding properties. They cannot be used to estimate non-use (option or existence) value, or to measure visitors' valuations. This can lead to gross undervaluations of environmental or historic conservation. The HPM framework is based on a number of restrictive assumptions: it is assumed, for example, that consumers are perfectly informed with respect to prices and attribute levels at all possible locations, and that a state of equilibrium exists in the housing market. In circumstances where these assumptions do not hold good, a valuation based on the HPM may be inaccurate to an unknown extent. Data requirements may also be onerous.

Further difficulties arise with regard to the actual estimation of the hedonic equation. These include bias from omitted variables, inappropriate functional form, and the presence of multicollinearity and market segmentation. These are viewed as serious drawbacks and are considered in turn below, as follows;

- *bias from omitted variables* In each study, the researcher must decide which variables are relevant for inclusion as regressors in the hedonic price equation. If a relevant variable is omitted, this will bias the coefficient estimate and hence subsequent valuations. Furthermore, Wilman and Perras (1989) have shown that omission of the price of a substitute or complement good in the hedonic regression will cause a further bias. Cheshire and Sheppard (1994) noted that it is 'important to have as fully specified a hedonic model as possible if robust estimates of housing characteristics… are to be derived.' This, in principle, was also a requirement if other types of building such as offices or retail premises were considered. They found that exclusion of any set of characteristic variables significantly changed the size of some of the coefficient estimates.

- *inappropriate functional form* As stated above, the appropriate functional form will be linear only in one special case. In most cases, a nonlinear form is preferable, but the nonlinearity could be one of many types.

- *multicollinearity* In order to avoid omitted variable bias, the researcher may include all variables that appear relevant. However, if included variables are very closely related (so that if one is present at a given property it is highly probable that the other is also), this will inflate the variances of the coefficient estimates, and could imply that none of the explanatory variables are significant, even though R^2 and the standard F-value may be high.

- *segmentation of markets* Treating housing markets which are in reality segmented (for example flats and detached houses, or historic and modern properties) as single markets will also lead to biased coefficient estimates in the hedonic regression. Failure to segment the markets in the estimation procedure would imply that parameters were forced to be constant across the sub-markets, a situation which is unlikely to occur in reality (Michaels and Smith 1990; Kanemoto and Nakamura 1986).

In a comprehensive study of various econometric problems associated with hedonic pricing, Graves *et al* (1988) showed that valuations of air quality differed significantly with functional form and estimation method, but only marginally with choice of measurement variable and measurement method.

The Travel Cost Method

The individual travel cost model (ITCM) can be written

$$V_{ij} = f(DC_{ij}, TC_{ij}, X_{ij}) \quad i=1, ..., r; j=1, ..., s.$$
(A1.3)

where V_{ij} is the number of visits by individual i to site j in a given period, DC are distance costs and TC time costs for visiting the site, and X is a vector of other variables (such as income, age, education, and trip details) which have explanatory power for V_{ij}. A zonal travel cost model (ZTCM) has also been developed, and is identical to that in (A1.3) except that the dependent variable becomes the number of visits made from a particular population zone i to the site j per 1000 of population in the zone. For ease of analysis, the zones are usually based on administrative districts with groups of postcodes, but they may also take the form of rings around the site, and in the case of linear resources such as waterways they may be rectangular (Harrison and Stabler 1981). The trip-generating function (TGF) is an equation which predicts how many trips an individual i will make to a site j in a given time period, and is given by (3.3). Alternatively, the zonal equivalent may be estimated using OLS. A demand curve for visits is then estimated for different travel costs. Total consumer surplus is calculated as the area between the cost of visits actually made and that cost which would force the number of visitors to zero. This is known as the 'added cost' method of constructing a demand curve for a specific site, as opposed to leisure travel on a particular trip.

In addition, Brown and Mendelsohn (1984) suggested a Hedonic Travel Cost Method (HTCM), a combination of hedonic pricing and travel cost analysis. In this case, the dependent variable was travel costs, and the independent variables were site attributes. In the first of two stages, the travel costs and time costs were regressed separately on the explanatory variables. In the second, a demand curve for each site characteristic was estimated by regressing its shadow price on the level of the attribute as well as other independent variables. Consumer surplus estimates could then be derived from the aggregate demand function for each site attribute.

Problems with the Travel Cost Method
A major drawback of the Travel Cost Method, as of HPM, is that only user values can be estimated. Clearly, the groups of users in a TCM study will be different from those in a hedonic study. In the case of the Travel Cost Method, the valuations of visitors to a recreational site who are both residents of and visitors to the area will be taken into account. By definition, those who do not visit the site (either because they are non-users or simply because they do not visit during the sample time) are assigned a zero valuation, even though they may be willing to pay to preserve the site (option and existence values). A primary methodological difficulty is the choice of either a zonal or individual formulation of the TGF. There appear to be no theoretical grounds for preferring one to the other, and a number of studies have found considerable differences in valuations between the two (Willis and Garrod 1991; Garrod and Willis 1991b). Hellerstein (1992) argued that zonal models may be superior to individual ones because they do not depend on any distributional assumptions.

Further difficulties arise in establishing the true purpose of the journey (Cheshire and Stabler 1976), in the treatment of recreationists who visit multiple sites, and in the analysis of holidaymakers compared with local residents. The first problem requires the researcher to classify visitors, perhaps arbitrarily, according to the prime objective of their outing. The second is to assign a certain proportion of the total travel cost to each site, although it may be possible to question people as to the relative importance of each destination. The third problem requires the researcher to decide whether to include only the (relatively small) daily travel costs of visiting a site or to add the cost of travelling to and from the holiday destination. Since it is likely that the holiday destination will have been chosen with the existence of nearby recreational sites in mind, failure to apportion some of this cost of travelling to each daily trip will lead to a significant site undervaluation. A further difficulty arises because many people who live in an area of historic or architectural significance, and thus incur a low measured travel cost, may have moved there precisely because they wanted to be close to a particular environmental site.

How to measure distance costs is also an issue. Should the researcher calculate spending on petrol alone, or incorporate an additional allowance for depreciation, road tax, and other running costs? How should time be valued: at the marginal wage rate of the visitor, or at the opportunity cost of alternative leisure pursuits foregone? The case of visitors who walk to a site and hence incur no travel costs is especially problematic.

Finally, statistical difficulties need to be considered. Bateman *et al* (1992) argue that multicollinearity between site attributes used in the TGF may lead to insignificant coefficient estimates. Various functional forms are again possible, including linear, quadratic, semi-log, and double-log models. There is no consensus among authors about which is preferable. In some cases, the functional form is such that the demand curve is asymptotic, or in other words if it does not intersect the axes. This occurs if there are extreme outliers either in the number of visits or the distance travelled (and hence the travel cost incurred), and raises the issue of whether, or where, to use cut-off points.

Since an on-site survey, by definition, will not capture individuals who do not visit the site during the sample period, the truncation at zero of non-visitors could bias consumer surplus estimates, resulting in an under-estimation of consumer surplus. Smith and Desvouges (1986) showed that in this case, the coefficient estimates will be biased under OLS so that the method of maximum likelihood (ML) must be used.

The Contingent Valuation Method

The CVM is a survey-based methodology, with responses obtained either by questionnaire or by interview. Telephone interviews are generally avoided, since it may be difficult to elicit an adequately informed response over the telephone, and the sample which can be contacted may be biased. Mail surveys are popular, but non-response biases or low response rates may be a problem. There are a number of stages involved in implementing the survey, the first of which is to set up a hypothetical reason for payment or compensation in the eyes of consumers. So, for example, respondents may be told that the government is considering clearing and improving a nearby canal and towpath, but only if additional funds are raised. The respondent is then informed about how much additional revenue is required, and how the scheme would be funded (the bid vehicle), for example by a local income tax or an entry fee.

Individuals are then questioned by the various means which have been developed within the method on their maximum WTP to ensure the project goes ahead, or on their minimum WTA compensation for the loss of the project. The actual bid figure may be obtained in one of four ways:

- *interactive bidding* The interviewer starts by suggesting an opening bid. If the respondent is willing to pay, the bid is increased and the question posed again; if the respondent is not willing to pay, the bid is reduced and the question posed again. This continues until the maximum WTP is derived.

- *a payment card* The respondent is given a card with a number of different payment values, from which he or she may choose one.

- *a dichotomous choice or referendum question* The respondent is simply shown one amount and asked whether he or she would be willing to pay that amount or not. Different respondents are presented with different amounts.

- *an open-ended question* No suggestions are given to the respondent, who is asked to choose his or her own maximum WTP with no prompting.

The last method is usually the least preferred, since respondents may have little experience in the valuation of such non-market goods, and may therefore find it difficult to reach a value which reflects their true WTP without any suggestions. Boyle and Bishop (1988) compared the first three payment formats, and concluded that no method was universally superior (a result echoed by Garrod and Willis 1992 and Jordan and Elnagheeb 1994). They argued that the iterative bidding method is likely to suffer from a starting-point bias, that the payment card method may suffer from an anchoring bias, but is likely to discourage protest bids, and that while the dichotomous choice approach is the simplest to administer, transforming a qualitative response into a monetary valuation requires advanced statistical techniques.

After the removal of any strategic or protest bids from the sample, average WTP estimates are calculated. The final steps in the analysis involve the estimation of a bid curve and aggregation of the sample mean WTP estimate to the population as a whole, however this is defined. Calculation of the bid curve involves a regression of the WTP/WTA on a range of explanatory variables which are thought to affect the bid and on which information has been elicited in the survey, for example incomes and educational levels. The parameter estimates from the bid curve are used to adjust the sample mean WTP to order to account for systematic differences between, for instance, income levels between the sample and population as a whole, prior to aggregation.

Problems with the Contingent Valuation Method
The CVM is possibly the least theoretically rigorous, and certainly the least developed of the valuation methods considered so far. Garrod and Willis (1990) made an extensive survey of many biases or errors which may be inherent in CV studies. Some of the most important are strategic bias, hypothetical bias, mental account bias, and biases resulting from survey design, as follows:

- *strategic bias* This may result from free riding, that is the deliberate misrepresentation of respondents' own WTP/WTA in order to serve their own interest. If consumers think that the improvement will go ahead irrespective of their answer, and that their payment could be based upon the valuation they give in the survey, they will have an incentive to understate their valuation. This problem can be overcome by stating that all consumers will pay the average bid.

- *hypothetical bias* Consumers may respond very differently to questions on a hypothetical situation from the way in which they would to those which refer to a real event. This could lead to random errors (Mitchell and Carson 1989). A misvaluation may occur if the respondent gives ill thought-out responses because he or she finds the situation difficult to relate to, or fails to take the survey seriously. Researchers therefore need to make the issue and the means of dealing with it as realistic as possible.

• *mental account or part-whole bias* This is apparent when the respondent appears to value large differences in environmental quality almost identically. This is explained by the observation that when individuals are asked to take part in a number of Contingent Valuation surveys, their total WTP may take up a large portion of their income, or even exceed it. Asked about one specific issue, they often allocate their whole environmental budget to it, because they are unaware of other possible environmental improvements toward which they might be willing to contribute. It is therefore necessary to try to establish the total environmental perception of individuals. Boyle *et al* (1994) tested for the presence of part-whole bias in a study of willingness to pay to prevent wildfowl deaths. They found that part-whole bias was evident, since a 100-fold increase in the number of birds saved led to only a very modest increase in willingness to pay. They concluded that this makes it extremely difficult to arrive at marginal valuations of changes in the quality or quantity of natural resources using the Contingent Valuation Method.

• *temporal embedding* This may occur when a respondent appears unable to distinguish between a willingness to accept payment in compensation for being denied one visit to a site and a willingness to accept payment for the permanent removal of the possibility of ever visiting that site.

• *biases resulting from survey design* A number of biases may result from the way in which the questions are phrased and the survey is implemented. Starting-point bias occurs when the the starting value suggested under the iterative bidding technique affects the final bid offered by the respondent, who may think that it is the sum which he or she should be willing to pay. The method of payment proposed in the survey may also influence the WTP/WTA figure given. For example, it has been found in a number of applications that willingness to pay via a sales or income tax was greater than that via an entrance fee. Hanley and Spash (1993) suggested that choosing non-controversial payment systems of the type most likely to be used in practice would improve the credibility of the results.

Production Function Methods

The basis of Production Function approaches is that firms and households combine factors of production and commodities respectively with environmental services in order to produce other goods and services. If the quality or quantity of an environmental attribute falls, economic agents such as holidaymakers will need to change their expenditure patterns in order to compensate.

Many authors (for example, Bateman, Garrod and Willis 1992) regard the TCM as simply one type of Production Function methodology, but there are other specific Production Function approaches, namely dose-response functions and avoided cost methods, which cannot be perceived as such.

• *dose-response functions* These are generally applied to the effect of changes in environmental quality on crop yields. A change in pollution levels may cause farm production to alter, and thus the financial effect of changes in the quality of environmental services can be measured and quantified.

• *avoided cost methods* The basis of the avoided cost method is that economic agents may be able to undertake an averting expenditure to minimise the effect of a fall in environmental quality. For example, if the quality of drinking water falls, households may purchase water filters. The sum of these expenditures by all affected parties could be viewed as a lower bound to an implicit valuation of the fall in water quality. Hansen and Hallam (1991), for example, used a production function approach to establish the relative value of an improvement in freshwater stream-flow to recreational fishing and to consumptive river uses such as agricultural irrigation. They found that marginal valuations of stream-flow changes were higher for recreational fishing than for their corresponding use in agriculture.

Averting expenditure, however, may only provide imperfect substitutes for the lost environmental service. Many people may not consider such expenditure (which may have a high threshold) worthwhile. As a result, valuations using avoided cost methods may produce underestimates; this has been found to be the case in many human life valuations (Dickie and Gerking 1991; Dardin 1980).

The Delphi Technique

Instead of attempting to ascertain the WTP of individuals (who may be irrational, impulsive, or poorly informed) for an environmental improvement, or their willingness to accept a degradation, it is possible to elicit the views of a panel of 'experts' on the valuation of environmental changes. The technique was developed by the RAND Corporation in the 1950s (Dalkey and Helmer 1963), and is found to be particularly useful in cases where historical data are unavailable or where significant levels of subjective judgement would be necessary (Smith 1989).

Essentially, the method consists of the researcher assembling a panel of experts who are believed to have some knowledge concerning the issue at hand. It is important that the panel be drawn from diverse fields, with different approaches, and therefore different viewpoints and subjective valuations. Panels have ranged in size from 4 (Brockhoff 1975) to 904 (Moeller and Getty 1974).

The next stage is the administration of a questionnaire, which gives the panel information on the study and asks for their valuation. The responses are then analysed, and then returned to the panel members, who are asked if they wish to update their valuation in the light of the other responses. The process of analysis, distribution of results, and re-questioning will occur at least one more time before final valuations are reached; in some cases a fourth or even a fifth round of questionnaires may be desirable. It is hoped that by this time there will have been some convergence of views between the experts in the light of discussions with their colleagues.

One advantage of the method is that it requires little specialist statistical knowledge, and is relatively simple to conduct, although the selection of an appropriate panel and the design and wording of the questionnaire may have a crucial influence on the final outcome. Some may also consider the process of valuation by so-called experts undemocratic and artificial.

Appendix 2 Abstracts of significant sources

Sources which are fully discussed in the body of the report are not generally included in this section.

Anderiesen and Reijdorp 1991 used interviews with residents in the historic centres of Amsterdam and Rotterdam to evaluate the outcomes of a housing rehabilitation programme. The residents reported that the housing had improved while the quarter had deteriorated. This was explained by the inadequate provision of services, and insufficient public consultation during and after rehabilitation. The authors concluded that the results of urban rehabilitation could not be understood if its objectives were not compared with an evaluation by the resident population. The qualitative assessment of housing rehabilitation was not examined, and was presented as unproblematic.

Andersson 1994 empirically tested the validity of using only one employment centre in determination of household bid-rent curves. A Hedonic Price (HP) regression approach was used, incorporating variables for structural attributes as well as incomes, local income tax rates, and other variables on a sample of 466 property prices for the region of Malmö-Lund, Sweden in 1990. He concluded that the monocentric model performed significantly better than a polycentric model in this case, but noted the significance of excluding relevant neighbourhood variables in determining coefficient estimates.

Asabere *et al* 1989 showed that architectural style has a strong impact on residential property valuation. They estimated a Hedonic Price Model on a sample of 500 properties sold in the Newport area of Massachusetts between 1983 and 1985. Older styles of architecture commanded premium prices. The paper also tested for the effect on valuation of historic zoning of the town. Their finding was that properties inside the historic region did not seem to command significantly higher prices than those outside.

Atkinson and Crocker 1992 used Bayesian methods to test the transferability of hedonic price functions (either in their entirety or for particular characteristics) across sites and time. They found that while valuations of structural housing characteristics were generally transferable, those of neighbourhood characteristics were not. They argued that this was to be expected since housing attributes are created by the building industry and will be priced at some function of cost in the market, while the supply of neighbourhood attributes is essentially fixed in time.

Bartik 1987 suggested that from an econometric viewpoint, estimation of hedonic demand parameters was not a normal identification problem. A new approach, based on instrumental variables, was needed.

Bartik 1988 argued that a measure of the value of amenity improvements from HP models by WTP of households originally at the improved site will underestimate potential benefits due to movement of housing consumers and suppliers. The paper proposed the use of extrapolated property values from the original hedonic equation in order to estimate the benefit, since no further data and little additional computation would be required.

Bateman *et al* 1992 This extensive survey charted the history and development of the Travel Cost Method (TCM) from its conception to the numerous possible formulations used today. It highlighted a number of recent applications, and mentioned some of the problems which may occur during its implementation.

Bateman *et al* 1993 compared a number of Contingent Valuation (CV) studies undertaken in the UK following a brief theoretical account of the development of Contingent Valuation Method (CVM). The study then focused on two studies in particular.

Bloomquist and Worley 1981 used a two-stage hedonic price of characteristics approach to estimate the demand curve for a number of urban amenities. They found that using a power transformation of the variables (with the variables raised to the power 0.1) performed better than the traditional linear formulation. Demand findings were calculated by regressing the quantity of each trait on its own price, prices of other traits, and income and preference variables.

Boer *et al* 1991 stated their finding of the superiority of the contingent ranking method over the traditional CVM for the valuation of the Amazon rain forest. They explained the intuition and theory behind contingent ranking, but failed to explain how to derive total benefit from the rankings.

Boyle *et al* 1994 empirically tested for the presence of part-whole bias in a CV study of WTP by non-users to prevent wildfowl deaths. They concluded that part-whole bias is important and makes marginal valuations of changes in quality or quantity of natural resources extremely difficult.

Boyle and Bishop 1988 compared the CV techniques of iterative bidding, payment cards and dichotomous choice. They concluded that none of these methods of eliciting consumer surplus was universally superior. The iterative bidding method was likely to suffer from a starting point bias; the payment card method might still suffer from an anchoring bias, but was likely to discourage protest bids. The dichotomous choice approach was simpler to use, but transforming a qualitative response into a monetary valuation required advanced statistical techniques.

Brooks and Young 1993 This paper presented the goals and strategies of downtown revitalisation pursued by the City of New Orleans between 1973 and 1993. The impacts of the growth management programme were reviewed, with special attention paid to four geographical areas. The authors noted that while the creation of the programme required the active participation of a coalition of government and business leaders, an increasing number of decisions were being made by the private sector in terms of the economic future of downtown New Orleans. The article concluded that the attempts to create a vibrant downtown produced few winners and many losers. The authors drew on reports prepared by the Downtown Development District as the basis of his conclusions, although a detailed examination of these reports was not presented in the article.

Brookshire and Crocker 1981 gave a sketchy outline of their views of why CVM is superior to other methods of non-market valuation.

Calthorpe Estate 1995 A submission was made describing this 3700-hectare estate, which was largely situated within a conservation area and contained approximately one third of all Birmingham's listed buildings. Conservation policies played a large part in the estate's activities and were seen as a major constraint because they increased maintenance costs and restricted the redevelopment of property which was not achieving its maximum potential. The estate's submission argued that the local planning authority had little regard for the adverse financial implications of conservation policies, particularly when compared to these parts of the estate which lay outside the conservation area.

Cambridge City Council 1995 This submission drew attention to the case study of St Andrew the Great, a church surplus to the needs of the Church of England, which had found a new religious use with the assistance of grant aid after planning consent for commercial adaptation was refused. Attention was drawn to market resistance to the listing of property and to procedures such as certificates of immunity to allow owners to protect their investment in property. The Cambridge submission drew attention to the fact that only 2 of the city's 700 listed buildings charged visitors an entry fee, and as a result their owners did not receive financial support for conservation. The Council sought a common basis for understanding the financial impact of conservation controls.

Cameron 1992 used CVM and TCM jointly to estimate the parameters of the demand and underlying utility functions for access to fishing water. She argued that the TCM showed current behaviour while CVM indicated likely future behaviour. Thus the two methods could be viewed as complementary. A further benefit of using both methods was that they could both be employed on the same sample.

Can 1990 showed that a spatially lagged house price equation could explain variations in house prices better than an HP model, and hence that the prices of houses are raised if they are close to higher-priced housing, irrespective of the structural condition of the houses in question. The paper concluded that the fit of hedonic models could be much improved by incorporating spatial lags into the estimated equations.

Carson and Mitchell 1993 argued that the oft-quoted lack of sensitivity of CV estimates to the characteristics of the good may pose a large problem for the methodology, since estimates for similar environmental changes have had wide-ranging valuation. They also stressed that quality of response is dependent upon the quality of information provided and the seriousness with which the subject takes the survey.

Caulkins *et al* 1986 showed that different assumptions with respect to decision-making by consumers affect the valuation of changes in site quality. They estimated a multinomial logit model of travel cost which explicitly accounted for consumers' substitution between sites as a result of changes in the quality of one site. Hence they argued that the traditional model which ignores substitution effects will over-value site quality improvements.

Cheshire and Sheppard 1994 used locational as well as structural characteristics in a hedonic price regression of the price of housing in Reading and Darlington in 1984. They concluded that it was 'important to have as fully a specified a hedonic model as possible if robust estimates of housing characteristics... are to be derived.' They found that exclusion of any set of characteristic variables significantly changed the size of some of the coefficient estimates.

Cheshire and Stabler 1976 argued that the Clawson assumption that journey time represents a cost rather than a benefit may not always be the case, since people on recreation may derive pleasure from the journey itself as well as the activity.

Cicchetti and Wilde 1992 This brief paper summarised early theoretical work on non-use values and CVM.

Cicin-Sain 1980 The purpose of this chapter was threefold. First it reviewed the scant empirical evidence available on the process of neighbourhood revitalisation, focusing on its incidence, characteristics, and human dimensions. Second, it set forth an analytical framework for considering the potential or hypothetical consequences of revitalisation on affected parties. While costs and benefits were identified only in conceptual and hypothetical terms (given the absence of data), this exercise was presented as being useful insofar as the mix of costs and benefits of revitalisation was likely to vary according to whose perspective was being considered. Third, the chapter considered the evidence available on the most negative aspect of revitalisation, the displacement of lower income residents from their neighbourhoods. The chapter concluded that revitalisation and its attendant consequences did not seem to represent a quantitatively significant phenomenon, and that displacement should be viewed as a national issue and a local problem.

City of Canterbury Planning Department 1975 This report described the results of a survey of tourist expenditure in Canterbury. The majority of visitors were reported as being attracted by the historic built form, while the use of *ad hoc* surveys for estimating tourist expenditure and employment generation was treated as unproblematic.

Civic Trust 1992a This study by the Civic Trust of the Brigg Regeneration Project set out the benefits of a broadly based conservation project with a financial statement of the costs, achievements, and the broader economic and social benefits to the area.

Civic Trust 1992b This study of Ilfracombe by the Civic Trust and North Devon District Council described the way in which a series of conservation initiatives jointly funded by local and national sources have sought to overcome local economic difficulties following the decline of established industries. The study identified local benefits and the coordination of a range of projects to provide a critical mass of projects to stimulate economic regeneration. It recognised the limitations of the programme in overcoming major economic constraints related to the location of Ilfracombe and economic changes in the holiday industry.

Combs *et al* 1993 used a matching grants approach to the contingent valuation of improved park facilities. A WTP of approximately $8 was estimated, which was more than double the tax increase necessary to cover the cost of the project.

Coursey and Schulze 1986 argued that the 'current inaccuracy of hedonic and travel cost approaches for valuing public goods' implied that a series of initial laboratory experiments was the best way to design a CVM survey.

Cropper *et al* 1988 considered how the form of the HP function could affect errors in estimation of marginal attribute prices. When all attributes were observed, linear and quadratic Box-Cox formulations fitted best, while if some attributes were unobserved or only proxied, linear and linear Box-Cox functions gave the best results in terms of having the minimum mean percentage error for the characteristic valuation (semi-log and log-log forms were also considered).

Crouter 1987 used the HP method to evaluate the efficiency of a regional water rights market in the US.

De Klerk and Vijgen 1994 The research compared the behaviour of different types of households living either within the inner city areas of Amsterdam and Rotterdam or elsewhere. Both of these inner city areas were being planned as public and cultural areas. The research used four indicators of city-centred *v* home-centred lifestyles: restaurant visits, museum card ownership, visits by and to family, and ownership of a video recorder. The results pointed to two diverging roads of urbanisation. In Amsterdam the inner city formed a lively public and cultural arena. A high level of urban amenities was sustained by a substantial number of people attracted to an urban way of life. In Rotterdam, the stock of human and physical resources was far weaker, and apparently insufficient to start a comparable structure.

Dickie and Gerking 1991 estimated WTP for atmospheric ozone reduction using a discrete choice adaptation of the production function approach. They found extremely high WTP figures — at least twice the value of savings in medical expenses that would result from the same proportionate reduction in ozone.

Do *et al* 1994 tested the effect of local churches (which have both positive and negative external qualities) in San Diego using a hedonic approach. They found that proximity to a neighbourhood church had a strong impact on house prices. The price effect was negative, and declined nonlinearly as distance increased.

Dobbs 1993 argued that many TCM studies suffered from sample-selection bias. That is, no information about non-users can be obtained from an on-site survey (truncation bias), which will also capture a larger than proportionate number of high-frequency visitors relative to the total number of visitors (endogenous sample-selection bias). Dobbs suggested a possible adjustment to TCM to take these possible biases into account, and then applied the new methodology to the valuation of forest recreation. He concluded that the extent of the bias will depend crucially on the functional form of the TC equation, with a linear model more severely affected than a semi-log form.

Dodgson and Topham 1990 examined how close residential property valuations from the Hedonic Pricing Method are to those of professional valuers on a range of properties from London and the north-west of England. The outcome was that the results were very closely matched, with only one major divergence in a sample of 32. They concluded that the hedonic method in general provides a useful way to value a number of properties of specific types or in specific areas.

Donaldson 1992 This highly theoretical paper considered the strengths and weaknesses of valuations based on four different measures of well-being, namely WTP, money metrics, extended money metrics, and welfare ratios. Donaldson concluded that WTP measures were highly problematic because 'the social binary relations lack ordinal rationality properties,' and that rankings are therefore inconsistent.

Edinburgh Old Town Renewal Trust 1995 This submission described the project, one of 18 co-financed by the European Commission as part of the Conservation of European Cities Programme, with the objective of providing expertise on the best use of Europe's historic cities to realise economic development. The submission identified the role of tourism and cultural activities within a broad, sustainable local economy. It also assessed the impact of tourism expenditure, which led to the creation of more than 2300 permanent jobs as a result of a coordinated conservation strategy.

Elberle and Hayden 1991 provided a brief critique of TC and CV theory, after noting the usual CVM biases. They were extremely critical of the CVM methodology, arguing that 'CVM is most likely to succeed where the operationalisation of the hypothetical market occurs...[but] when these conditions hold, it is also the case that there are other methods available in addition to CVM... Regardless of efforts to make [CVM] models more sophisticated, doubt remains as to whether these models will produce results that have meaning.' They concluded that neither CVM nor TCM 'can be legitimised in a theoretical sense from a neo-classical, psychometric or general systems point of view. The CV and TC approaches lack methodological, theoretical and empirical grounding. Their continued use will mislead valuation attempts and frustrate policy intended to restore a viable environment.' But the authors failed to suggest any alternatives.

Englin and Mendelsohn 1991 presented a hedonic travel cost model which was used to indicate the value of alterations in the quality of forest sites. They derived the Hedonic Travel Cost Method (HTCM) from the theory of utility maximisation, calculated compensation measures required for a change from the current level of the characteristic to zero, and provided estimates of the user value from US data.

Ford 1989 evaluated the effect of historic district designation on the prices of a sample of properties sold in Baltimore, Maryland between 1980 and 1985. Using HP, she found that historic designation had a positive but insignificant effect on the prices of these houses.

Forrest 1991 used region-categorised HP models to estimate regional differences in house prices (represented by the coefficient on the constant term in the hedonic regression), when allowing for differences in housing structural attributes across regions. Their conclusion was

that regional differences may be significantly over- or under-stated when these variations in characteristics are not allowed for.

Freeman 1979 gave a guide to the theoretical underpinning and assumptions involved in the use of hedonic price equations for property values, and concluded that although hedonic pricing was theoretically rigorous, it involved many abstractions from the data.

Freeman 1991 developed three categories of model to evaluate the benefits of changes in environmental risks from economic theory.

Gale 1991 compared the change in median professional valuations of properties before and after historic district designation for six study areas in Washington DC. His main finding was that 'this analysis of the residential historic district experience in Washington found no evidence that historic designation, *per se*, is associated with increases in property values out of proportion to the effects of generally prevailing economic conditions.' The rate of appreciation of housing values declined in all six areas under study, but valuations decreased by almost as much across the whole city. He concluded that designation had only an insignificant effect on residential property valuation. Evidence was also found that designated properties were insulated to a certain extent from general cyclical fluctuations in the economy. The author also claimed that existing research provided only a few insights into the displacement of low income and elderly households.

Garrod and Willis 1990 gave a useful review of the many sources of bias and error which may occur in CV studies.

Garrod and Willis 1991a aimed to value countryside characteristics using the HP method. They found that a number of environmental variables were not significant in their hedonic regression study of houses close to the Forest of Dean.

Garrod and Willis 1991b used both the individual and zonal Travel Cost Methods (ITCM and ZTCM respectively) to estimate the value of Forestry Commission land. They found huge differences between the valuations arrived at using the two methods, with the ITCM producing an aggregate valuation only 16% of that of the ZTCM.

Garrod and Willis 1992a considered the relative strengths and weaknesses of the four main methods for extracting contingent valuations in surveys, namely open-ended versus dichotomous choice question formats, payment cards, and iterative bidding. They argued that one could not state *a priori* which method is superior, but that the choice of method depended specifically on the study. But they did note that the payment card method was the least popular, and that dichotomous choice formats were preferred in mail-based surveys.

Garrod and Willis 1992b applied a Hedonic Pricing model to explore the impact of proximity to forests of various types on house prices, and to estimate the demand for certain types of woodland. They found that forestry may have a large impact on house prices. They highlight the problem of multicollinearity between different tree variables and additionally between housing structural attributes. They concluded that there was no incentive for Forestry Commission plantation, given the huge benefits that would accrue to private developers who set aside land for forestry, although many benefits may be external.

Garrod, Pickering and Willis 1991 used a travel cost approach to the valuation of four botanic gardens. The results showed that consumer surplus (or aggregate willingness to pay response to a single CV question) was considerably lower (10–15%) than the total cost to the state, in terms of grant aid, of the upkeep of the gardens.

Garrod, Willis and Saunders 1994 used CVM to value the Somerset Levels and Moors Environmentally Sensitive Area (ESA) scheme. They found that user value was around six times the cost to the state of ESA designation. Non-user value was also high (22 times its cost).

Gleye 1988 argued that the US program of tax breaks for rehabilitation of historic buildings, while contributing to urban regeneration, may have proved detrimental to the very buildings it was intended to preserve. The paper, which was very specific to the American case, suggested a number of changes to the policy which might better protect the buildings.

Graves et al 1988 investigated the effect of the econometric problems of variable selection, measurement error, functional form, and distributional assumptions on hedonic valuations of air quality. They found that valuations differed significantly with functional form and estimation method, but only marginally with choice of measurement variable and measurement method.

Graves and Knapp 1985 showed that hedonic valuations of many amenities tended to understate systematically their true values. They looked at the effects of amenity changes on the interaction between the housing and labour markets. The study provided a good introduction to HP, but did not take the analysis much further.

Green et al 1994 examined the robustness of responses in a Contingent Valuation study to slight changes in the wording of the question. The study asked visitors to a museum of science in California to give their WTP for teaching English to immigrants and for saving birds from oil leaks. Valuations were considerably reduced when the issue of increased taxation was broached. Serious sampling biases were likely to have resulted from their choice of base for questioning.

Green and Tunstall 1991 argued that many problems, both theoretical and empirical, still remained unsolved in the non-user valuation of non-market goods. They considered the relative importance of various reasons for positive non-use valuations and surveyed various theoretical issues.

Hanley 1988 briefly described the three main methods for valuing non-market goods. A CV study was then undertaken to value a ban on the burning of straw.

Hanley and Craig 1991 estimated, by CVM, preservation benefits to users and non-users of the Flow Country in Scotland. One-off mean WTP to preserve was found to be approximately £17. Aggregated across the whole Scottish population, this gave an estimate of total benefit of £68 million. The Krutilla-Fisher model was also used in order to quantify the irreversibility of wilderness development. They concluded that 'on efficiency grounds, there seems to be no justification for subsidising further aforestation.'

Hanley and Ruffell 1992 used both the TCM and CVM to evaluate consumer surplus across different types of forestry, each with different physical characteristics. The TC study showed a strong relationship between visits per year and mean height of trees, reason for visit, length of stay, and importance of visit. Most characteristics were insignificant in the regression and this was attributed to poor measurement of characteristics. The CV analysis revealed wide variations in WTP by cause of visit.

Hanley and Ruffell 1993 used two contingent valuation estimation approaches to value the physical characteristics of forests in the UK. They found that forest characteristics provided a poor explanation of willingness to pay (WTP). The mean WTP varied significantly by purpose of visit, and ranged from approximately 60p to £1.50 per visit.

Hanley and Spash 1993 This book is an excellent introduction to, and critique of, HPM, TCM, CVM, and other methods of valuation.

Hanna and Binney 1978 This study surveyed a wide collection of historic villages, towns, gardens and cathedral cities. The aim of the research was to evaluate the effectiveness of a conserved built environment in attracting tourists, and to value the economic benefits resulting from this tourist activity. Shopowners were asked questions concerning the impact of tourism on their business, which they were reported as finding hard to assess. Overall, the range and number of locations in which interviews were undertaken did not make up for the lack of rigour in the approach.

Hansen and Hallam 1991 used a production function approach to the valuation of recreational fishing benefits relative to consumptive river usages such as agricultural irrigation. They used a maximum likelihood procedure to estimate a tobit regression model which has as its dependent variable the number of days spent freshwater fishing per year. They concluded that marginal values of stream-flow changes were higher for recreational fishing than for their corresponding use in agriculture.

Harrison and Stabler 1981 used TCM to measure the amenity values of canals in the UK. They interviewed 848 people over nine sites. One result was the finding that visitors' income was the main determinant of both the method of travel and the distance travelled, independent of the recreational activity or cost of it. Clawson's assumption that consumers were indifferent to the distinction between leisure travel costs and other costs (such as entry fees) was refuted.

Harrogate Borough Council 1995 Harrogate Borough Council and the North Yorkshire County Council outlined the benefits to Ripon of a coordinated conservation strategy, following work with the Civic Trust and other organisations interested in the future of the town. The project drew attention to the critical mass required to improve the local economy and the opportunities for improvement based upon a conservation strategy. Tourism played an important part.

Hellerstein 1992 argued that if non-participants were not properly treated in travel cost models, the results would be biased. Ideally a stratified sample of the general population should be used, but since this was unlikely to yield a sufficiently high number of users, on-site surveys were often used instead. Zonal models might be superior to individual ones, since they did not depend on any distributional assumptions.

Hoehn et al 1987 developed a general hedonic multi-market model for the study of inter-regional wages, house prices, and location-specific amenities.

Horowitz 1993 offered some Bayesian perspectives on the Contingent Valuation Method.

Hough and Kratz 1983 argued that architecture has certain public good characteristics which may be undervalued in the marketplace. They estimated a hedonic regression with architectural quality as an independent variable. Their major finding was that office tenants were prepared to pay a premium for new buildings with high values of architectural quality, but were not willing to pay a similar premium for old buildings of comparable architectural stature.

They concluded that, while the market would ensure a supply of good new architecture, old buildings had to be protected in some way since they were undervalued in the market for office space.

Hubbard 1993 provided a critical review of behavioural research on conservation. The author noted that although arguments had been put forward in support of the psychological and aesthetic value of the conserved environment, there was still very little certain knowledge of people's conscious or unconscious commitment to buildings from the past or to those being constructed today. As a consequence, 'conservation remains shackled by the stigma of subjectivity and accusations of élitism.' Contemporary approaches to conservation tended to treat townscapes as art rather than as a setting for everyday life. An understanding of how people look at, make sense of, and generally feel about, the conserved environment was a prerequisite for the development of a coherent theoretical basis for conservation policy and practice.

Jordan and Elnagheeb 1994 conducted experiments to determine if there was any difference between WTP estimates arrived at using each of two question formats commonly employed in CVM: referendum (dichotomous choice) or payment cards. When strategic bias was controlled, neither method of questioning significantly outperformed the other, but the payment card method generally had lower mean square-error.

Kahneman and Ritov 1994 measured respondents' WTP for interventions into various environmental or public health problems after being shown brief 'headline' statements, rather than the general and lengthy introduction generally given in CVM questionnaires. Unsurprisingly, they found strong correlations between the strength of the respondents' view of the importance of the problems and their WTP.

Kain 1982 This article described the application of the Malraux Act in France. The author provided reference to other studies (Soucy 1974 and 1976) in order to argue that in terms of social dislocation, many rehabilitation schemes were no less disruptive than urban renewal. The author commented on the prospects for the *Operations programmées d'amélioration de l'habitat.*

Kanemoto 1988 demonstrated theoretically that the Hedonic Pricing Method overvalued amenities in public project evaluation, so that valuations should be used only as an upper bound to the true valuation. But, as the author noted, the paper assumed perfect, costless mobility between regions; if this were relaxed, the conclusion might be reversed.

Kanemoto and Nakamura 1986 illustrated that one difficulty with HP estimation was that within the market as a whole there are many different sub-markets, each with its own characteristics. There are rarely sufficient data to estimate separate structural equations. They therefore suggested a new estimation method which would overcome this difficulty.

Kanmein 1993a found that sequential CV studies could improve the efficiency of WTP estimates relative to traditional one-off studies, since the former could allow for informed bid updating. They found, using Monte Carlo experimental techniques, that up to four stages might significantly improve estimation.

Kanmein 1993b considered the issue of the optimal choice of bid values for the double-bonded logit model, and derived a number of rules.

Kask and Maani 1992 gave an HP model which accounted for informational awareness and the level of uncertainty among consumers when valuing non-market goods. They showed, both theoretically and empirically, that poorly informed consumers will give biased HP estimates. Information had the effect of changing subjective valuations and probability estimates in uncertain situations, with the direction of bias depending upon the level of information and uncertainty involved.

Kealy *et al* 1990 tested the reliability and validity of CVM by estimating WTP valuations for two goods at opposite ends of the private-public good spectrum, namely a chocolate bar and the alleviation of acid rain in a recreational area. They found that the nature of the good may have little influence, and that scepticism about the validity of the technique for valuing environmental goods with which consumers were not familiar was not substantiated by the evidence.

Kealy and Turner 1993 found by experiment that WTP for a public good depended on whether the questions were open- or closed-ended. This was not the case with private goods. One suggested explanation was that the closed format prevented strategic behaviour, although their study indicated that neither method was always superior.

King and Sinden 1988 used HP to measure the effect of soil conservation on farm land values. They concluded that there was a strong positive relationship between land quality and its price, and that land conservation appeared to be fully valued in the marketplace.

Larson 1992 a and b showed theoretically a number of consequences of substitution relationships between market and public goods for the user and non-user valuation of public goods.

Larson 1993 asked whether existence value could, as traditionally supposed, be measured only by CVM. Larson dismissed models which gave rise to pure

existence values as special cases unlikely to occur in reality. He also argued that existence value may in principle be measured from observing demand behaviour as well as from CVM, although, disappointingly, the paper did not attempt to suggest how this might be achieved.

Lazo *et al* 1992 offered a psychologist's perspective on how contingent valuations might be obtained for non-users of an environmental good.

Legal & General Assurance Society Limited— Millbank Tower 1995 Following the seminar, the Legal & General provided copies of their correspondence with the Department of National Heritage on the adverse economic impact of the listing of modern buildings. They sought to draw attention to the difference between the economic life and the aesthetic value of a building. Legal & General's case was based upon the assumption that buildings, including modern office developments, have a useful life, and that once they have reached the end of it they have little economic potential.

Linneman 1980 surveyed some procedures for estimating HP functions for housing, indicating a number of possible biases. An empirical investigation found that neighbourhood-specific characteristics could explain up to 50% of the variation in valuations between structurally identical housing.

Lockwood *et al* 1993 used a dichotomous choice CV survey to assess WTP to preserve national parks in Victoria, Australia. They used a logit regression model to estimate the respondents' probability of being prepared to pay. The sample estimate of $AUS52 was aggregated to the whole population of Victoria. Assuming non-respondents to have zero WTP and adjusting individual WTP to take into account differences in socio-economic characteristics between the sample average and the population, this yielded a value of $AUS14m. The CV survey revealed the relative importance of existence and bequest values. They concluded that continued timber harvesting 'does not constitute a socially optimal or economically efficient allocation of resources.'

Loomis 1987 argued that the method used for generalising sample results to total population valuations could considerably alter the final outcome. He argued that a weighted approach which accounted for sampling bias should be used. Low income, low education groups, for example, would otherwise be under-represented, with the result that the project would be overvalued.

Loomis *et al* 1991 suggested a method for determining whether benefit estimates from CVM and TCM are statistically significantly different. Estimates of valuations of WTP for Californian deer hunting for the two methods were found to differ considerably in the mean, although the 90% confidence intervals did overlap, indicating that differences found in other studies may not be as statistically significant as they appeared.

Lopez *et al* 1994 argued that land used for agricultural purposes may have important amenity benefits which are often not reflected in allocation of agricultural land.

Maani and Kask 1991 used the Hedonic Pricing Method to estimate house purchasers' WTP to avoid a high-pressure gas line being installed in their vicinity. The WTP was reflected in the additional expenditure the consumer was willing to make on a comparable property outside the hazardous area. They concluded that, when there is no certainty that the hazard will occur, HPM may under- or over-estimate the WTP, particularly if consumers are poorly informed or influenced by biased media reports.

Marcus 1995 The paper reviewed the concept of estate management schemes created under the provisions of the Leasehold Reform Act, including conservation areas. The author compared the impact of estate management schemes with conservation area designation.

Mattson and Li 1994b reported that in two successive CV mail surveys of WTP for visits to Swedish forests, they found no significant non-response bias in attitudes and valuations.

McConnell 1992a argued that if both the HP and TC methods are used to value environmental damage, the total damage is not the sum of these components, since there will be some common element. This was due to the fact that expected future benefits of close proximity to an environmental amenity, as well as the recreational value, were already incorporated in local house prices.

McConnell 1992b argued that the cost of on-site time should be taken fully into account in the TCM, as has rarely been the case. Furthermore, on-site time should be modelled endogenously. Estimation of the demand curve and subsequent valuations remained unchanged.

McPherson 1992 used a 'greenspace accounting' approach to the valuation of benefits and costs of a tree planting program in Tucson, Arizona. A money value was placed on the positive environmental externalities produced by trees (for example shading and cooling of buildings, storm water soaking, and pollution fixing), so that the possible benefits of tree planting could be assessed in the context of the costs and benefits of other forms of investment in urban infrastructure.

Mendelsohn *et al* 1992 argued that TCM studies have traditionally ignored trips with multiple destinations. They suggested that multiple-site trips should be viewed as visits to additional sites. That is, combinations of destinations should be treated as separate sites and included in a demand system. Consumer surplus estimates for multiple destination trips were found to be approximately 60% higher on average than those for single destinations.

Michaels and Smith 1990 argued that a single hedonic price equation will not in general adequately model the complex relationship between the price of housing and its characteristics. They implemented the analysis of separate sub-markets, each with individual HP equations.

Moorhouse and Smith 1994 valued nineteenth-century terraced houses in Boston, Massachusetts using HP. The properties were similar in layout, but differed substantially in architectural design. Their major finding was that, when other factors were accounted for, there was a premium on individuality and certain styles. The regression was statistically significant, and variables had their expected signs.

Navrud 1991 tested the validity of CVM by investigating whether people would indeed pay the amount they had stated in their valuation. Respondents were asked to give their willingness to pay to preserve biodiversity, and their true WTP was related to whether they were prepared to (and did) pay to join the WWF. Less than a third of those who responded with positive WTP actually paid the fee. The author concluded that most respondents understood the WTP question as one of general rather than monetary support, and that this may be viewed as a general problem for CVM studies.

Neyret 1992 The first part of this book presented a series of papers from prominent academics and professionals advising on projects aimed at the conservation of the cultural built heritage. The economic and social benefits of conservation were heralded, with reference to a range of cities including Boston, Philadephia, Charleston, New Orleans, Strasbourg, Lyon, Bologna, Paris, and Québec. These papers presented qualitative assessments of the value of conservation, which found a limited degree of support in the short case studies which comprised the second half of the book. Overall, the collection of papers suggested that the consequences of conservation will depend on the socio-economic conditions prevailing at the time, and the degree of political commitment to the stated objectives of conservation.

Nijkamp and Bithas 1995 The report of this case study used non-economic measurement units as well as qualitative information, as intended supplements to traditional economic methodology, in the assessment of sustainable monument planning in Olympia, Greece. The authors proposed a decision-making framework which incorporated the interests of different social groups in the form of different rankings of relevant decision criteria.

Palmquist 1982 proposed a new technique, the resale technique, for the valuation of changes in environmental attributes of housing. The prices of given houses were tracked over time as they were resold, and changes in environmental characteristics over the time period were quantified. This technique overcame a number of problems associated with the traditional HP method (such as specification of functional form), but presented a number of new ones (such as the necessity of the properties having been traded at least twice, and that no significant changes (such as internal structural alterations) had occurred, other than those in measured environmental variables.

Patin 1988 This study described the economic fringe benefits generated by 13 French monuments receiving 200,000–250,000 visitors per year. It concluded that financial outlay on the conservation of an architectural monument enhanced its value, and that visitors spent four times their entrance fee on meals, accommodation, etc. In cases where a monument was one destination among others, such analysis was problematic.

Pearce 1994 highlighted the importance of historic conservation as a means to urban regeneration. The study outlined a number of reasons why conservation might have this effect: it demonstrated commitment, enhanced the image of a town, improved business confidence, encouraged tourism, and increased the quality of housing. The quality of the environment was seen as an important influence on the choice of business location.

Pennington et al 1990 estimated the effect of proximity to an aircraft flight path on the HP valuation of housing in Stockport. They found that noise had a modest (6% on average) negative influence on housing values, but when all other neighbourhood characteristics were accounted for, the difference in values was insignificant. They concluded that the sample of properties close to the flight path would probably have lower values even without the airport. One important contribution of the paper was the specification of the number of bedrooms and the number of living rooms as separate 0/1 dummy variables, in order that the marginal valuation on an additional bedroom or living room need not be constant.

PIEDA/DoE 1995 assessed the impact of Environmental Improvement Projects (EIP), including the extent to which these projects achieved economic regeneration objectives. The study reviewed a wide range of projects in the UK including conservation-related schemes such as the Lace Market in Nottingham, and concluded that EIPs can make a practical contribution to urban renewal in attracting and supporting private investment. The report stateds that the impact of EIPs was substantially influenced by economic circumstances, market conditions, and physical constraints. The report believed that EIPs assisted regeneration but did not have the capacity to completely overcome major constraints such as location or adverse market conditions. This study highlighted the use of project feasibility studies and the early identification of expected achievable market objectives with a review of the objectives actually achieved, including the relationship between private and public funding.

Prince et al 1992 demonstrated by the use of laboratory-type experiments that the contribution game mechanism of CV can be used to reduce strategic bias and problems associated with price anchoring.

Punter 1991 This article evaluated the success of one of the first long-term conservation programmes launched by a British city, in Bristol. It gave an account of the initiatives, progress, and achievements of the programme. While noting that an objective measurement of the environmental quality of the programme was impossible, the author drew on the opinions of local property agents. In response to critics who argued that the conservation programme's achievements were due to market trends, the author noted that the programme led rather than followed the recovery in the property market. Furthermore, the programme had had to overcome significant budgeting difficulties, which restricted the local authority's social goals of providing low cost housing.

Randall 1994 argued that the costs of travelling to recreational sites was not really known, since these costs were by definition unobservable. The best that could be achieved from a TC study, therefore, was an ordinal ranking of alternatives.

Salokangas 1995 This paper reported on two research projects undertaken in Finland on the cultural built heritage. The first study concluded that the reuse of industrial buildings was costly if the new use was not in balance with the nature of the old building. The relative utility of space in the old industrial buildings was found to be less than in their modern equivalents, in part due to the running costs (including heating, cleaning, and maintenance). The second study pointed to the employment generation effects of conservation, but noted that tax regulations made conservation more costly.

Shaeffer and Millerick 1991 studied the impact of National Historic District Designation on four areas around Chicago. A hedonic pricing approach was followed on a total of 252 properties spread across the four areas. They found that designation had a significant positive effect on property prices.

Smith 1979 reviewed and assessed the means developed in Charleston, South Carolina, of conserving the city's architectural heritage. The first section outlined the history of the development of Charleston. The subsequent sections examined the role of zoning in protecting the city's historic centre and the important part played by voluntary associations. Recent developments in neighbourhood rehabilitation were discussed, together with fiscal measures to encourage rehabilitation. The author noted that the relative success of housing rehabilitation in the six-block Ansonborough section had encouraged other housing improvements in midtown Charleston, although a detailed assessment was not provided.

Smith 1984 This thesis examined aspects of conservation programme implementation in Norwich, UK. It addressed the issue of property values in relation to demand for housing and shop units. This assessment was inconclusive and lacked rigour. The author provided a number of pointers on the difficulties associated with defining and collecting information on tourists.

Smith 1992 gave a critical appraisal of a paper by Kahneman and Knetsch (1992) in which they conducted two telephone surveys in Vancouver to investigate the effect of commodity description, payment terms, and question sequences on elicited CVM valuations. He argued that all Kahneman and Knetsch's conclusions were dubious and that, contrary to their report, their responses could be rationalised by standard economic theory.

Smith and Kaoru 1987 gave a general overview of HTCM methodology. They argued that HTCM could not be viewed as a simple extension of the general HP framework since a number of additional assumptions were necessary.

Smith *et al* 1991 estimated the TC function for each user as a technically efficient frontier. They tested the theory on the results of a survey to value improvements in the quality of fishing in the Albermale-Pamlico Estuary, North Carolina. The frontier HTC performed considerably better that standard OLS estimates.

Spilsbury 1992 provided case study material on the way in which three properties in or near London (Merton Abbey Mills, Richmond, and Shad Thames) have provided data as the basis of an appraisal of the economic and social benefits derived from their conservation and reuse. The thesis suggested a framework for the analysis of the heritage benefits.

Spitalfields Historic Buildings Trust 1995 This submission drew attention to the fact that the property market could have long lead times and was also influenced by fashion, so that historic buildings, including those owned by the public sector, could be undervalued at certain times. The Trust drew attention to buildings' potential to act as catalysts for the redevelopment of larger areas, with broader benefits.
Stébé 1995 This article was solely interested in the evaluation act and its stakes, with rehabilitation as the

example. From 33 evaluation studies, selected from the total numbers of studies identified in France, the following characteristics were examined: *post hoc* examination, lack of distance, self-prescription, plurality of conceptions, methodological weaknesses (principally with regard to imprecision, data availability, and rigour), atomised references, and self-justification. The analysis showed that the studies were carried out with the essential goal of learning and understanding, and not with a cognitive and operational perspective. Under these conditions, the evaluation act closes the process of rehabilitation instead of participating in its evolution.

Thayer 1981 theoretically and empirically investigated the importance of various biases in a CV study of WTP to prevent geothermal energy sites being installed in an area. He found that starting point bias, hypothetical bias, and information bias were all insignificant in their influence on WTP.

Thomas 1983 examined a series of case studies in order to demonstrate that the coordination of resources was a central objective of planning in residential conservation areas. The case studies were used in order to support the original hypothesis, and did not provide rigorous links between the objectives of 'planning' and policy outcomes in residential conservation areas.

Triplett 1986 discussed the way in which various aspects of HP models, such as hedonic functions and implicit prices, could be interpreted in intuitive terms.

Triplett 1992 followed the history of the development of hedonic models.

Van Duren 1993 examined changes in the retail trade, and in restaurant and café activities, in order to assess the revival of Amsterdam city centre, the changed nature of its attraction, and the people it attracted. The author noted certain limitations on the use of available floorspace data in the Netherlands. The data on the supply of commercial consumer services did not unequivocally indicate a rising trend. The author concluded that part of the confusion about whether the attraction of the city centre was increasing sprang from the fact that the area harbouring consumer-oriented activities was expanding towards its edges. The author also emphasised that it was not so much the amount but rather the character of supply that had changed. This was due to changes in the composition of the visitors, which was confirmed by a study of the population of a specific street.

Williams 1980 This paper made a preliminary evaluation of the *Comissariado para la renovacão da area Ribeira-Barredo* (CRUARB). The author criticised the project in Oporto, Portugal, on three counts: its slow rate of progress, its anti-democratic mode of operation, and its lack of powers in the field of employment. On the positive side, the project demonstrated that although high-quality renovation is expensive, it need not be prohibitively so in comparison with renewal. The author noted that CRUARB had succeeded to a considerable extent in combining the aims of housing improvement, architectural conservation, and cultural renovation, although a detailed account was not provided.

Willis 1989 gave a rare treatment of the explicit contingent valuation of option value (OV). In a survey of WTP to preserve various Sites of Special Scientific Interest (SSSI), option value was found to be between 10% and 20% of the total site valuation. The author concluded that although option value could be measured by CVM, the existing literature had devoted insufficient time to explaining the factors influencing the OV for individuals.

Willis, Beale, Calder and Fleet 1993 assessed the usefulness of the CV method for estimating WTP to gain access to Durham Cathedral. They considered CVM to be a 'consistent, robust and efficient estimator' of WTP. They argued that a voluntary charge would yield a higher revenue than a fixed entrance charge, although utility measured through WTP was almost twice the average contribution paid. Non-use value (that is, option and existence value) were unfortunately not considered in the survey, since only those already visiting the cathedral were questioned.

Willis and Garrod 1990 considered the effect of selection bias from the exclusion of non-users on valuations obtained by the TCM in a study of canals in the UK. They found the bias to be less important than that arising from an inappropriate functional form. On the whole, they concluded, consumer surplus estimates were considerably larger than government subsidies to British Waterways Board, although there were wide variations between individual canals.

Willis and Garrod 1991a compared estimates of consumer surplus for visits to various forest sites derived from the ITCM and ZTCM. The ZTCM had the weakness that individual consumers' WTP was not calculated, and that the number of visitors per 1000 of population was very small in some cases. The ITCM estimates were considerably smaller than those from the ZTCM, and also smaller than those obtained from one CV question on the TC questionnaire.

Willis and Garrod 1993b used both HP and CV methods to estimate the benefits of canals. Non-response in the CVM method was approximately 40%. The CVM study produced far higher valuations for proximity to the waterside. A number of reasons for this were suggested.

Willis, Garrod and Dollis 1990 used ITCM to value recreational benefit derived from the Lancaster and Montgomery Canals. In neither case was the consumer surplus estimate sufficient to cover the huge financial loss in operating the canal, although the authors noted that their estimates provided a lower bound on total consumer surplus, and that the canal produced other non-measured benefits which were not incorporated into the study.

Willis, Garrod, Saunders and Whitley 1993 surveyed a number of methods for valuing the benefits of the Environmentally Sensitive Areas (ESA) scheme, including Household Production Function (HPF), HP, CVM, and TCM. They concluded that TCM might be better able to value specific recreational sites than general landscape areas. HP might be unable to separate the effect of ESA designation from the value which would have existed anyway. They suggested that CVM was the preferable method, since it allowed both use and non-use values to be estimated.

Wilman and Perras 1989 argued that the price of a substitute or complement site (in the eyes of consumers) should be included as a regressor in TC equations, as omission would bias the estimated coefficients, and hence the corresponding consumer surplus estimate.

York Consulting Ltd and Centre for Urban Development and Environmental Management 1993 This study assessed the Calderdale Inheritance Project, a ten-year multi-faceted programme which sought to enhance key areas in order to stimulate reinvestment and regeneration. The plurality of methodological approaches utililsed in the assessment uncovered a broad range of impacts, summarised under the following headings: economic change, investment and conservation, and image and confidence. Overall, by reviewing aims, methods used, resources deployed and attracted, benefits secured, lessons learned, and case studies to illustrate findings, the study went beyond being a purely descriptive account to provide an operational perspective of use to a wide audience.

Appendix 3 Summary of the proceedings of the seminar held in London on 9 June 1995

Christopher Penn, a partner at Jones Lang Wootton, Chartered Surveyors, opened the afternoon's proceedings from a commercial perspective. Although conscious 'that we derive our identity and sense of belonging…' from our heritage, which formed 'the very foundation of any civilised society,' he felt that it was under threat from misguided planning policies. These emphasised only the benefits of conservation, instead of taking an even-handed approach that also counted the costs. There was, in his view, a 'loss to society as a whole… in terms of jobs, taxes, environment, and infrastructure improvements… as a result of restrictive planning policies'. He called for compensation for the loss of development rights as a result of conservation policies, for maintenance costs of historic buildings to be free of VAT, and for greater distinction to be made between residential and commercial buildings. He also commented on the protection that listing placed on interiors as well as exteriors, and hoped that the implementation of PPG 15, of which he was in favour, would bring a greater flexibility in decision-making. He hoped that future research would deal with these issues (although they were practical ones faced by property professionals), rather than focusing on valuation methodologies which sought to improve understanding of the impact of conservation policies.

Geoffrey Wilson, an English Heritage Commissioner and a developer himself, felt that Christopher Penn's arguments were too strong. Conservation could work with development, resulting in sensitive and appropriate refurbishment. He felt that sometimes the broader benefits of conservation were not fully recognised.

Sarah Higgins, Conservation Officer, Ryedale District Council, said that local planning authorities would be aided in their work and decision-making if the value of conservation could be demonstrated more readily.

David Burns suggested that future research should focus on York, Chester, Chichester, and Bath. Studies undertaken there in the 1960s (for example, Buchanan and Partners 1968 for Bath) were worth reviewing. He was critical of the lack of quantitative data on the nature of the built heritage in this country.

Michael McCarthy, Pegasus Retirement Homes (developers of the Empire Hotel, Bath), felt that conservation projects would be greatly encouraged if developers were given more support from the public sector to 'help hedge against the risk'; 5% or 10% public support might make many projects commercially viable.

David McLaughlin, Conservation Officer, Bath City Council, argued that the existing designation processes were effectively a system of identifying cultural value. He also emphasised that conservation should be a dynamic process; it was concerned with guiding change, not preventing it.

Francis Carnwath, Chairman, the Spitalfields Trust, spoke in some detail about how active conservation could provide the nucleus for an area's regeneration. Often, however, it required a determination to overcome prevailing circumstances and attitudes. He mentioned an individual property which, having been written off by the market, had been repaired and was now a landmark building, creating value around it.

Nat Litchfield, Planning Consultant, focused his remarks on what he called 'the decision-making process', where purely financial considerations were often of little help. Central to that was the use of cost-benefit analysis. He argued that by using it *ex ante*, a choice between options could be made which would maximise the values one is seeking to favour. Through an *ex post* approach, which allowed monitoring, comparisons could be made with the predicted outcome. His work on the 'planning balance sheet' tried to understand the impact of decisions in terms of the broader community. He recognised that the key ambition was to get 'surrogate values' in order to put value on things that the market does not normally value. The biggest problem was that 'there is no common language'; however, cost-benefit analysis came closest by 'the cost-benefit family of methods'.

Rosemarie McQueen, Conservation Officer, Westminster City Council, argued that cities could thrive through well considered conservation policies. She cited the fact that Westminster had entertained representatives from 12 different countries over the previous year, with the purpose of learning from their conservation policies.

Gregory Beecroft, British Rail Property Board, and so concerned with disused railway structures, cast some doubt on finding the 'real' willingness to pay, but felt it could be a useful means of measurement if its problems were resolved.

Jenny Page, Chief Executive of the Millennium Commission, had been previously involved with the research and felt that the key issue was to find 'a language in which we can genuinely communicate with a wider audience'. She questioned the pressures from the commercial sector for 'large floor plate… modern, hygienic space', since most of the activity was at the small business end of the market, and many nineteenth-century buildings provided the seedbed in which those enterprises could start.

Colin Redman, Grosvenor Estate and RICS, called for some focus in the discussion. One aspect that all had to recognise was that conservation was successful when it generated use and amenity. To arrive at a true understanding of the value of conservation, a holistic approach was necessary, and that should be reflected in future case studies.

Jack Warshaw, Conservation Architecture and Planning, felt that there were a number of mythologies existing about conservation, in particular that it imposed restrictions and froze action. He added that the 'so-called restrictive planning system actually gave rise to that excellent development' at Broadgate. He complained about the lack of quantitative material regarding grade II buildings and conservation areas in this country, which hampered the development of effective policies. He finished with an interesting and commonly uttered remark, that 'the wealthy are more likely to pay for a good environment than the non-wealthy.' This was worth investigating: 'it could be the other way around.'

Katherine Scanlon, University of Cambridge and author of earlier research into the economic effects of listing (Scanlon *et al* 1994), raised the issue of compensation. She pointed out that owners tended to bear the cost of conservation measures, while others reaped the benefits. Conservation policies might be rational from an economic point of view, since their total benefits probably outweighed their cost; but were they fair?

Peter Nijkamp, Professor of Urban Economics, Free University of Amsterdam, gave a thorough analysis of the literature review and the methodologies that had been identified. He outlined some of the problems of valuation in the field of conservation through a number of witty anecdotes which enabled many in the audience to understand the concepts more clearly. He felt that in conservation planning, the focus should not be on the assessment of absolute or relative values without comparing alternative choice possibilities; a shadow price was needed. Many of the approaches identified in fact raised more potential problems than solutions. Values were determined by many different criteria depending on whose viewpoint was being considered, which was why information on the asset was so important. He offered a step-by-step process which involved some awareness of institutional input which helped to shape the climate in which values were determined. He finished by suggesting that some lessons could be learnt from environmental economics, which was now an established discipline, and that a portfolio of cases needed to be compiled.

Chris Green, Chief Executive, English Heritage, closed the seminar by emphasising that in conservation, as in investment in public transport infrastructure, the benefits woud always be more difficult to quantify than the hard costs. Nonetheless, we must attempt to get closer to being able to do so. He felt that the next step should be to apply what has been learnt through the study to developing a robust methodology for case studies, which English Heritage and others could then apply to the evaluation of key projects with which it was involved.

Bibliography

Abelson, P W, and Markandya, A, 1985 The interpretation of capitalised hedonic prices in a dynamic environment, *Journal of Environmental Economics and Management* **12**, 195–206

Adamowicz, W L, Bhardwaj, V, and Macnab, B, 1993 Experiments on the difference between willingness to pay and willingness to accept, *Land Economics* **69 (4)**, 416–27

Adger, N, and Whitby, M, 1991 National accounting for the externalities of agriculture and forestry, *Countryside Change Unit Working Paper 16*, Department of Agricultural Economics and Food Marketing, University of Newcastle-upon-Tyne

Adger, N, and Whitby, M, 1990 Appraisal and the public good: environmental assessment and cost-benefit analysis, *Countryside Change Unit Working Paper 7*, Department of Agricultural Economics and Food Marketing, University of Newcastle-upon-Tyne

Agnus, J M, 1985 *Economie du patrimoine: resources economiques engendrées par la patrimoine monumental — le cas du Mont Saint Michel*, Ministère de la Culture, Paris

Allenbenefoti, P G, Stevens, T H, and Barrett, S A, 1981 The effect of variable omission in the travel cost technique, *Land Economics* **57 (2)**, 173–80

Ambrose, P, 1994 *Urban process and power*, Routledge, London

Anderiesen, G, and Reijdorp, A, 1991 *Le restrutturazioni urbane e le loro implicazioni sociali: i casi di Amsterdam e di Rotterdam* (Urban revitalisation and its social implications: the cases of Amsterdam and Rotterdam) in *Le transformazioni sociali dello spazio urbano* (ed P Petsimeris), 203–221, Patron Editore, Bologna

Andersson, D A, 1994 Households and accessibility: an empirical study of households' valuation of accessibility to one or more concentrations of employment services, *University of Reading, Department of Economics Discussion Paper Series C 8 (97)*, Reading

Archer, B, Shea, S, and De Vane, R, 1974 *Tourism in Gwynedd: an economic study*, report to Wales Tourist Board by Institute of Economic Research, University College of North Wales, Bangor

Asabere, P K, Hachey, G, and Grubaugh, S, 1989 Architecture, historic zoning, and the value of homes, *Journal of Real Estate Finance and Economics* **2**, 181–95

Ashworth, G, and Tunbridge, J E, 1990 *The tourist historic city of London*, Belhaven

Atkinson, S E, and Crocker, T D, 1992 The exchangeability of hedonic property price studies, *Journal of Regional Science* **32 (2)**, 169–83

Balkan, E, and Khan, J R, 1988 The value of changes in deer hunting quality: a travel cost approach, *Applied Economics* **20**, 533–9

Barbier, E B, 1994 Valuing environmental functions: tropical wetlands, *Land Economics* **70 (2)**, 155–73

Bartik, T J, 1987a Estimating hedonic demand parameters with single market data: the problems caused by unobserved tastes, *The Review of Economics and Statistics* **69**, 178–80

Bartik, T J, 1987b The estimation of demand parameters in hedonic price models, *Journal of Political Economy* **95 (1)**, 81–8

Bartik, T J, 1988 Measuring the benefits of amenity improvements in hedonic price models, *Land Economics* **64 (2)**, 172–83

Bateman, I, 1991 Social discounting, monetary evaluation and practical sustainability, *Town and Country Planning* **60 (6)**, 174–6

Bateman, I, Garrod, G, and Willis, K, 1992 An introduction to the estimation of the benefits of non-priced recreation using the travel-cost method, *Countryside Change Unit Working Paper 36*, Department of Agricultural Economics and Food Marketing, University of Newcastle-upon-Tyne

Bateman, I, Willis, K, and Garrod, G, 1994 Consistency between contingent valuation estimates: a comparison of two studies of UK National Parks, *Regional Studies* **28 (5)**, 457–74

Bennett, J, and Carter, M, 1991 Recent developments in contingent valuation studies in Australia, paper presented to the Second Annual Meeting of the European Association of Environmental and Resource Economists, Stockholm

Berrens, R, Bergland, O, and Adams, R M, 1993 Valuation issues in an urban recreational fishery: Spring Chinook salmon in Portland, Oregon, *Journal of Leisure Research* **25 (1)**, 70–83

Bishop, K D, and Stabler, M J, 1991 The concept of community forests in the UK: the assessment of their benefits, paper presented to the Second Annual Meeting of the European Association of Environmental and Resource Economists, Stockholm

Bloomquist, G, and Worley, L, 1981 Hedonic prices, demands for urban housing amenities, and benefit estimates, *Journal of Urban Economics* **9**, 212–21

Boer, I de, Folmer, H, and Prince, R, 1991 The contingent ranking method, paper presented to the Second Annual Meeting of the European Association of Environmental and Resource Economists, Stockholm

Bohm, P, 1972 Estimating demand for public goods: an experiment, *European Economic Review* **3**.

Bougarel, G, 1992 *Le patrimoine condamné par l'economie liberale?* in *Le patrimoine à tout du developpment* (R Neyret), 77–81, *Collection Transversales II*, 77–81, Université de Lyon, Lyon

Bowker, J M, and MacDonald, H F, 1993 An economic analysis of localised pollution: rendering emissions in a residential setting, *Canadian Journal of Agricultural Economics* **41**, 45–59

Boyle, K J, and Bishop, R C, 1988 Welfare measurements using contingent valuation: a comparison of techniques, *American Journal of Agricultural Economics* **70**, 21–8

Boyle, K J, Desvouges, W II, Johnson, F R, Dunford, R W, and Hudson, S P, 1994 An investigation of part-whole biases in contingent valuation studies, *Journal of Environmental Economics and Management* **27**, 64–83

Bravi, M, and Lombardi, P, 1994 *Techniche di valutazione* (Techniques of valuation), Celid, Turin

Brockhoff, K, 1975 The performance of forecasting groups in computer dialogue and face to face discussion, in *The Delphi method: techniques and applications* (eds H A Limestone and M Turoff), 291–321 Addison-Wesley, Reading, Massachussetts

Brooks, J S, and Young, A H, 1993 Revitalising the central business district in the face of decline: the case of New Orleans, 1973–1993, *Town Planning Review* **64** (6), 251–72

Brookshire, D S, and Crocker, T D, 1981 The advantages of contingent valuation methods for benefit-cost analysis, *Public Choice* **36**, 235–52

Brookshire, D S, Thayer, M A, Schulze, W D, and D'Arge, R C, 1982 Valuing public goods: a comparison of survey and hedonic approaches, *American Economic Review* **72**, 165–77

Brown, G Jr, and Mendelsohn, R, 1984 The hedonic travel cost method, *Review of Economic Studies* **66**, 427–33

Buchanan, C and Partners 1968 *Bath: a study in conservation*, HMSO, London

Buckley, M, 1988 Multicriteria evaluation: measures, manipulation and meaning, *Environment and planning B: planning and design*, **15** (1) 55–64

Burman, P, Pickard, R, and Taylor, S, 1995 *The economics of architectural conservation*, University of York, York

Burrows, G S, 1968 *Chichester: a study in conservation*, HMSO, London

Cameron, T A, 1992 Combining contingent valuation and travel cost data for the valuation of non-market goods, *Land Economics* **68** (3), 302–17

Calthorpe Estate 1995 *A submission to DTZ Debenham Thorpe on the value of conservation dated 22 September 1995*. (A description of the adverse impact of conservation policies on the estates property in Birmingham including a comparison with their properties outside conservation areas.) Unpublished

Cambridge City Council 1995 *A submission to DTZ Debenham Thorpe dated September 1995*. (A review of the effect of conservation in Cambridge and the potential for historic buildings to find new financially viable uses.) Unpublished

Cameron, T A, 1992 Nonuser resource values, *American Journal of Agricultural Economics* **74**, 1133–7

Cameron, T A, 1991 Interval estimates of non-market resource values from referendum contingent valuation surveys, *Land Economics* **67** (4), 413–21

Cameron, T A, and James, M D, 1987 Efficient estimation methods for 'closed-ended' contingent valuation surveys, *Review of Economics and Statistics* **69**, 29–276

Can, A, 1990 The measurement of neighbourhood dynamics in urban house prices, *Economic Geography* **6**, 254–72

Carson, R T, and Mitchell, R C, 1993 The issue of scope in contingent valuation studies, *American Journal of Agricultural Economics* **75**, 1263–7

Catt, R, 1991 Few guidelines to putting a price on architectural history, *Chartered Surveyor Weekly* **36**, 18–19

Caulkins, P P, Bishop, R C, and Bouwes, N W Sr, 1986 The travel cost method for lake recreation: a comparison of two methods for incorporating site quality and substitution effects, *American Journal of Agricultural Economics* **68**, 291–7

Cheshire, P C, and Sheppard, S, 1994 On the price of land and the value of amenities, *Economica* **62**, 247–67

Cheshire, P C, and Stabler, M J, 1976 Joint consumption benefits in recreational site 'surplus': an empirical estimate, *Regional Studies* **10**, 343–51

Cicchetti, C J, and Wilde, L L, 1992 Uniqueness, irreversibility, and the theory of non-use values, *American Journal of Agricultural Economics* **74**, 1121–5

Cicin-Sain, B, 1980 The costs and benefits of neighbourhood revitalization, in *Urban Revitalization 18* (ed D B Rosenthal), *Urban Affairs Annual Reviews*, Sage Publications, London

City of Canterbury Planning Department 1975 *Tourist Study*, Canterbury

City of Edinburgh District Council Planning Department 1995 *Action Plan Review*, Edinburgh

Civic Trust 1992a *Brigg Regeneration Project*, London

Civic Trust 1992b *New heart for Ilfracombe*, London

Clawson, M, and Knetsch, J.L, 1966 *The economics of outdoor recreation*, Johns Hopkins University Press, Baltimore

Coccossis, H, and Nijkamp, P, 1995 *Planning for our cultural heritage*, Aldershot

Colardelle, M, 1992 *La dimension economique du patrimoine culturel* in *Le patrimoine a tout du developpment* (R. Neyret), 45–7, *Collection Transversales II*, Université de Lyon, Lyon

Combs, J P, Kirkpatrick, R C, Shogren, J F, and Herriges, J A, 1993 Matching grants and public goods: a closed-ended contingent valuation experiment, *Public Finance Quarterly* **21** (2), 178–95

Cooper, J, and Loomis, J B, 1992 Sensitivity of willingness to pay estimates to bid design in dichotomous choice models, *Land Economics* **68** (2), 211–24

Cordell, H K, and Bergstrom, J C, 1993 Comparison of recreational use values among alternative reservoir water level management scenarios, *Water Resources Research* **29** (2), 247–58

Council of Europe 1991 *Funding the architectural heritage*, Council of Europe, Strasbourg

Coursey, D L, Hovis, J L, and Schulze, W D, 1987 The disparity between willingness to accept and willingness to pay measures of value, *The Quarterly Journal of Economics* **102**, 679–90

Coursey, D L, and Schulze, W D, 1986 The application of laboratory experimental economics to the contingent valuation of public goods, *Public Choice* **49**, 47–68

Creigh-Tyte, S W, 1996 *Option appraisal of expenditure decisions: a guide for the Department of National Heritage and its non-departmental public bodies*, London

Creigh-Tyte, S W, forthcoming The development of British policy on built heritage preservation in *Economic perspectives of cultural heritage*, London

Crocker, T D, and Shogren, J F, 1991 *Ex ante* valuation of atmospheric visibility, *Applied Economics* **23**, 143–51

Cropper, M L, Deck, L B, Kishor, N, and McConnell, K.E, 1988 On the choice of functional form for hedonic price functions, *Review of Economics and Statistics* **70**, 668–75

Cropper, M L, Deck, L B, and McConnell, K E, 1993 Valuing product attributes using single market data: a comparison of hedonic and discrete choice approaches, *Review of Economics and Statistics* **75** (2), 225–32

Cropper, M L, and Oates, W E, 1992 Environmental economics: a survey, *Journal of Economic Literature* **30**, 675–740

Crouter, J P, 1987 Hedonic estimation applied to a water rights market, *Land Economics* **63** (3), **257–71**

Cummings, R G , Ganderton, P T, and McGuckin, 1994 Substitution effects in CVM values, *American Journal of Agricultural Economics* **76**, 205–14

Dalkey, N , and Helmer, O, 1963 An experimental application of the Delphi method of the use of experts *Management Sciences* **9** (3), 458–67

Daubert, J T , and Young, R A, 1981 Recreational demands for maintaining instream flows: a contingent valuation approach, *American Journal of Agricultural Economics* **63**, 666–76

Davis, O A, and Whinston, A B, 1961 The economics of urban renewal, in *Urban renewal: the record and the controversy* (ed J Q Wilson), Massachussetts

De Klerk, L, and Vijgen, J, 1994 Inner cities as a cultural and public arena: plans and people in Amsterdam and Rotterdam. *Built Environment* **18** (2),100–110

Dickie, M, and Gerking, S, 1991 Willingness to pay for ozone control: inferences from the demand for medical care, *Journal of Environmental Economics and Management* **21**, 1–16

Do, A Q, Wilbur, R W, and Short, J L, 1994 An empirical examination of the externalities of neighbourhood churches on housing values, *Journal of Real Estate Finance and Economics* **9**, 127–36

Dobbins, J C, 1994 The pain and suffering of environmental loss: using contingent valuation to estimate non-use damages, *Duke Law Journal* **43** (4), 879–946

Dobbs, I M, 1993 Adjusting for truncation and sample selection bias in the individual travel-cost method, *Journal of Agricultural Economics* **44** (2), 335–42

Dobbs, I M, 1991 The individual travel-cost method: estimation and benefit assessment with a discrete and possibly grouped dependent variable, *Countryside Change Unit Working Paper 17,* Department of Agricultural Economics and Food Marketing, University of Newcastle-upon-Tyne

Dodgson, J S, and Topham, N, 1990 Valuing residential properties with the hedonic method: a comparison with professional valuations, *Housing Studies* **5** (3), 209–13

Donaldson, D, 1992 On the aggregation of monetary measures of well-being in applied welfare economics, *Journal of Agricultural Economics* **17** (1), 88–102

Donnison, D, and Middleton, A (eds), 1987 *Regenerating the inner city, Glasgow's experience*, Routledge and Kegan Paul, London

Drury, P J, 1995 English Heritage's contribution to the debate in Burman, Pickard, and Taylor (eds), 19–25

Duffield, J W, and Patterson, D A, 1991 Inference and optimal design for a welfare measure in dichotomous choice contingent valuation, *Land Economics* **67** (2), 225–39

Eberle, W D, and Hayden, F G, 1991 Critique of contingent valuation and travel cost methods for valuing natural resources and ecosystems, *Journal of Economic Issues* **25** (3), 649–87

Edmonds, R G Jr, 1983 Travel time valuation through hedonic regression, *Southern Economic Journal* **50**, 83–98

Edwards, S F, and Anderson, G D, 1987 Overlooked biases in contingent valuation surveys: some considerations, *Land Economics* **63** (2), 168–78

Englin, J, and Mendelsohn, R, 1991 A hedonic travel cost analysis for valuation of multiple components of site quality: the recreational value of forest management, *Journal of Environmental Economics and Management* **21**, 275–90

Epple, D, 1987 Hedonic prices and implicit markets: estimating demand and supply functions for differentiated products, *Journal of Political Economy* **95** (1), 59–80

Esher, L 1968 *York: a study in conservation*, HMSO, London

Ford, D A, 1989 The effect of historic district designation on single-family home prices, *American Real Estate and Urban Economics Association (AREUEA) Journal* **17** (3), 353–62

Forrest, D, 1991 An analysis of house price differentials between English regions, *Urban Studies* **25** (3), 231–8

Freeman, A M III, 1979 Hedonic prices, property values and measuring environmental benefits: a survey of the issues, *Scandinavian Journal of Economics* **81**, 154–73

Freeman, A M III, 1989 Assessing damages from the Valdez oil spill, *Resources for the Future* **96**, 5–7

Freeman, A M III, 1991 Indirect method for valuing changes in environmental risks with non-expected utility preferences, *Journal of Risk and Uncertainty* **4**, 153–65

Gale, D E, 1991 The impacts of historic district designation: planning and policy implications, *Journal of the American Planning Association* **57** (3), 325–40

Garrod, G, and Allanson, P, 1991 The choice of functional form for hedonic house price functions, *Countryside Change Unit Working Paper 23,* Department of Agricultural Economics and Food Marketing, University of Newcastle-upon-Tyne

Garrod, G, Pickering, A, and Willis, K, 1993 The economic value of botanic gardens: a recreational perspective, *Geoforum* **24**, 215–24

Garrod, G, and Willis, K, 1990 Contingent valuation techniques: a review of their unbiasedness, efficiency and consistency, *Countryside Change Unit Working Paper 10,* Department of Agricultural Economics and Food Marketing, University of Newcastle-upon-Tyne

Garrod, G, and Willis, K, 1991a The environmental economic impact of woodland: a two stage hedonic price model of the amenity value of forestry in Britain, *Applied Economics* **24**, 715–28

Garrod, G, and Willis, K, 1991b The hedonic price method and the valuation of countryside characteristics, *Countryside Change Unit Working Paper 14,* Department of Agricultural Economics and Food Marketing, University of Newcastle-upon-Tyne

Garrod, G, and Willis, K, 1991c Some empirical estimates of forest amenity value, *Countryside Change Unit Working Paper 13,* Department of Agricultural Economics and Food Marketing, University of Newcastle-upon-Tyne

Garrod, G, and Willis, K, 1992 Elicitation methods in contingent valuation: open-ended and dichotomous choice formats, iterative bidding and payment card methods, *Countryside Change Unit Working Paper 28,* Department of Agricultural Economics and Food Marketing, University of Newcastle-upon-Tyne

Garrod, G, Willis, K, Saunders, C M, 1994 The benefits and costs of the Somerset Levels and Moors ESA, *Journal of Rural Studies* 10 (2), 131–45

Georgiou, S, 1994 Economic valuation of etrophication damage in the Baltic Sea region: a review of relevant valuation studies, reports for the CVM Network, Stockholm School of Economics, 10

German Commission for UNESCO 1980 *Protection and cultural animation of monuments, sites and historic towns in Europe,* Bonn

Gleye, P H, 1988 With heritage so fragile: a critique of the tax credit program for historic building rehabilitation, *Journal of the American Planning Association* 54, 482–8

Graves, P E, and Knapp, T A, 1985 Hedonic analysis in a spatial context: theoretical problems in valuing location-specific amenities, *Economic Record* 61, 737–43

Graves, P E, Murdoch, J C, Thayer, M A, and Waldman, D, 1988 The robustness of hedonic price estimation: urban air quality, *Land Economics* 4 (3), 220–32

Green, C H, and Tunstall, S M, 1993 The ecological and recreational value of river corridors: an economic perspective, paper presented at the international symposium 'The Ecological Basis for River Management', Leicester

Green, C H, and Tunstall, S M, 1991a Is the evaluation of environmental resources possible? *Journal of Environmental Management* 33, 123–41

Green, C H, and Tunstall, S M, 1991b The evaluation of river quality improvements by the contingent valuation method, *Applied Economics* 23, 1135–46

Green, D P, Kahneman, D, and Kunreuther, H, 1994 How the scope and method of public funding affect willingness to pay for public goods, *Public Opinion Quarterly* 58, 49–67

Greffe, X, 1990 *La valeur économique du patrimoine,* Economia, Paris.

Gregory, R, 1986 Interpreting measures of economic loss: evidence from contingent valuation and experimental studies, *Journal of Environmental Economics and Management* 13 (4), 325–37

Gregory, R, Lichtenstein, S, and Slovic, P, 1993 Valuing environmental resources: a constructive approach, *Journal of Risk and Uncertainty* 7, 177–97

Gregory, R, MacGregor, D, and Lichtenstein, S, 1992 Assessing the quality of expressed preference measures of value, *Journal of Economic Behavior and Organization* 17, 277–92

Hall, P, and Cheshire, P C, 1987 The key to success for cities, *Town and Country Planning* 56, 50–52

Halvorsen, R, and Pollakowski, H O, 1981 Choice of functional form for hedonic price equations, *Journal of Urban Economics* 10, 37–49

Hanemann, M, Loomis, J, and Kanninen, B, 1991 Statistical efficiency of double-bounded dichotomous choice contingent valuation, *American Journal of Agricultural Economics* 73, 1255–63

Hanley, N, 1988 Using contingent valuation to value environmental improvements, *Applied Economics* 20, 541–9

Hanley, N, and Craig, S, 1991 Wilderness development decisions and the Krutilla-Fisher model: the case of Scotland's 'Flow Country', *Ecological Economics* 4, 145–64

Hanley, N, and Knight, J, 1992 Valuing the environment: recent UK experience and an application to Green Belt land, *Journal of Environmental Planning and Management* 35 (2), 145–60

Hanley, N, and Ruffel, R, 1993 The contingent valuation of forest characteristics: two experiments, *Journal of Agricultural Economics* 44, 218–29

Hanley, N, and Ruffel, R, 1992 The valuation of forest characteristics, *Queen's Discussion Paper 849*

Hanley, N, and Spash, C L, 1993 *Cost-benefit analysis and the environment,* Edward Elgar, Aldershot

Hanna, M, and Binney, M, 1978 *Preservation pays,* SAVE Britain's Heritage, London

Hansen, L T, and Hallam, A, 1991 National estimates of the recreational value of streamflow, *Water Resources Research* 27 (2), 167–75

Harris, C C, Driver, B L, and McLaughlin, W J, 1989 Improving the contingent valuation method: a psychological perspective, *Journal of Environmental Economics and Management* 17, 213–29

Harrison, A J M, and Stabler, M J S, 1981 An analysis of journeys for canal-based recreation, *Regional Studies* 15 (5), 345–58

Harrison, G W, 1992 Valuing public goods with the contingent valuation method: a critique of Kahneman and Knetsch, *Journal of Environmental Economics and Management* 23, 248–57

Harrogate Borough Council 1995 *Conservation Area Partnership Action Plan,* Harrogate

Headicar, M E, 1994 *A methodology to evaluate the effectiveness of the urban development corporations:* Paper 3: Final Recommendations

Hellerstein, D, 1992 The treatment of non-participants in travel cost analysis and other demand models, *Water Resources Research* 28 (8), 1999–2004

Henderson, D M, Lee Cousins, R, Coppock, J T, Duffield, B S, Owen, M L, and Dowers, S, 1975 *The economic impact of tourism: a case study in Greater Tayside,* Tourism and Recreation Research Unit, University of Edinburgh, Edinburgh

Hendon, W S, Shanahan, J L, Hilhorst, I T H, and van Straalen, J, 1983 *Economics and historic preservation*, Akron, Ohio

Hoehn, J P, 1991 Valuing the multidimensional impacts of environmental policy: theory and methods, *American Journal of Agricultural Economics* 73, 289–99

Hoehn, J P, Berger, M C, and Bloomquist, G C, 1987 A hedonic model of inter-regional wages, rents and amenity values, *Journal of Regional Science* 27 (4), 605–17

Hoehn, J P, and Loomis, J B, 1993 Substitution effects in the valuation of multiple environmental programs, *Journal of Environmental Economics and Management* 25, 56–75

Horowitz, J K, 1993 A new model of contingent valuation, *American Journal of Agricultural Economics* 75, 1268–72

Hough, D E, and Kratz, C G, 1983 Can 'good' architecture meet the market test? *Journal of Urban Economics* 14, 40–54

Hubbard, P, 1993 The value of conservation: a critical review of behavioural research, *Town Planning Review* 64 (4) 359–73

Hughes, J, 1994 Antarctic historic sites: the tourism implications, *Annals of Tourism Research* 21 (2), 281–94

Insall, Donald W, and Associates 1968 *Chester: a study in conservation*, HMSO, London

Investment Property Databank 1993 *The investment performance of listed buildings*, Royal Institution of Chartered Surveyors and English Heritage, London

Investment Property Databank 1995 *The investment performance of listed buildings — 1994 update*, Royal Institution of Chartered Surveyors and English Heritage, London

Investment Property Databank 1996 *The investment performance of listed buildings — 1995 update*, Royal Institution of Chartered Surveyors and English Heritage, London

Jacques, S, 1992 The endowment effect and the Coase theorem, *American Journal of Agricultural Economics* 74, 1316–23

Johansson, P-O, 1990 Willingness to pay measures and expectations: an experiment, *Applied Economics* 22, 313–29

Johnson, F R, 1991 Measuring existence values: environmental altruism and the missing behavioural link, paper presented to the Second Annual Meeting of the European Association of Environmental and Resource Economists, June 10–14 1991, Stockholm

Jones, P J S, and Kerr, S, 1994 The potential role of environmental management and conflict resolution techniques in the coastal zone, paper presented at the Conference on Management Techniques in the Coastal Zone, Portsmouth

Jordan, J L, and Elnagheeb, A H, 1993 Willingness to pay for improvements in drinking water quality, *Water Resources Research* 29 (2), 237–45

Jordan, J L, and Elnagheeb, A H, 1994 Consequences of using different question formats in contingent valuations: a Monte Carlo study, *Land Economics* 70 (1), 97–110

Kahneman, D, and Knetsch, J L, 1992 Valuing public goods: the purchase of moral satisfaction, *Journal of Environmental Economics and Management* 22, 57–70

Kahneman, D, and Ritov, I, 1994 Determinants of stated willingness to pay for public goods: a study in the headline method, *Journal of Risk and Uncertainty* 9, 5–38

Kain, R, 1982 Europe's model and exemplar still? The French approach to urban conservation, 1962–1981, *Town Planning Review* 53, 403–22

Kanemoto, Y, 1988 Hedonic prices and the benefits of public projects, *Econometrica* 56 (4), 981–9

Kanemoto, Y, and Nakamura, R, 1986 A new approach to the estimation of structural equations in hedonic models, *Journal of Urban Economics* 19, 218–33

Kanninen, B J, 1993a Design of sequential experiments for contingent valuation studies, *Journal of Environmental Economics and Management* 25, S1–11

Kanninen, B J, 1993b Optimal experimental design for double-bounded dichotomous choice contingent valuation, *Land Economics* 69 (2), 138–46

Kask, S B, and Maani, S A, 1992 Uncertainty, information, and hedonic pricing, *Land Economics* 68 (2), 170–84

Kealy, M J, and Bishop, R C, 1986 Theoretical and empirical specifications issues in travel cost demand studies, *American Journal of Agricultural Economics* 68, 660–7

Kealy, M J, Montgomery, M, and Dovidio, J F, 1990 Reliability and predictive validity of contingent values: does the nature of the good matter? *Journal of Environmental Economics and Management* 19, 244–63

Kealy, M J, and Turner, R W, 1993 A test of the equality of closed-ended and open-ended contingent valuations, *American Journal of Agricultural Economics* 75, 321–31

Keeble, D, 1989 The dynamics of european counter-urbanisation in the 1980s: corporate restructuring or indigenous growth? *The Geographic Journal* 155 (1), 70–74

King, D A, and Sinden, J A, 1988 Influence of soil conservation on farm land values, *Land Economics* 64 (3), 242–55

Kling, C L, 1989 A note on the welfare effects of omitting substitute prices and quantities from travel cost models, *Land Economics* 65 (3), 290–6

Knetsch, J L, 1990 Environmental policy implications of disparities between willingness to pay and compensation demanded measures of values, *Journal of Environmental Economics and Management* 18, 227–37

Krupnick, A J, 1993 Benefit transfers and valuation of environmental improvements, *Resources for the Future* 110, 1–7

Lancaster, K J, 1966 A new approach to consumer theory, *Journal of Political Economy* 84, 132–57

Larson, D M, 1992a Can non-use value be measured from observable behaviour?, *American Journal of Agricultural Economics* 74, 1114–20

Larson, D M, 1992b Further results on willingness to pay for non-market goods, *Journal of Environmental Economics and Management* 23, 101–22

Larson, D M, 1993 On measuring existence value, *Land Economics* **69** (4), 377–88

Lazo, J K, Schulze, W D, McClelland, G H, and Doyle, J K, 1992 Can contingent valuation measure non-use values? *American Journal of Agricultural Economics* **74**, 1126–32

Legal & General Assurance Society Limited 1995 *A submission to DTZ Debenham Thorpe dated 19 September 1995*

Lichfield, N, 1956 *Economics of planned development*, Estates Gazette, London

Lichfield, N, 1988 *Economics in urban conservation*, Cambridge University Press, Cambridge

Lichfield, N, Hendon, W, Nijkamp, P, Ost, C, Realfonzo, A, and Rostirolla, P, 1993 *Conservation Economics*, International Council on Monuments and Sites (ICOMOS), Sri Lanka

Linneman, P, 1980 Some empirical results on the nature of the hedonic price function for the urban housing market, *Journal of Urban Economics* **8**, 47–68

Lockwood, M, Loomis, J, and DeLacy, T, 1993 A contingent valuation survey and benefit-cost analysis of forest preservation in East Gippsland, Australia, *Journal of Environmental Management* **38**, 233–43

Lombardi, P, and Sirchia, G, 1990 *Il quarterre 16 IACF di Torino*, in *Misurare nell'incertezza* (ed R Roscelli), Celid, Turin

Loomis, J B, 1992 The evolution of a more rigorous approach to benefit transfer: benefit function transfer, *Water Resources Research* **28** (3), 701–5

Loomis, J B, 1988 Contingent valuation using dichotomous choice models, *Journal of Leisure Research* **20** (1), 46–56

Loomis, J B, 1987 Expanding contingent value sample estimates to aggregate benefit estimates: current practices and proposed solutions, *Land Economics* **63** (4), 396–402

Loomis, J B, Creel, M, and Park, T, 1991 Comparing benefit estimates from travel cost and contingent valuation using confidence intervals for Hicksian welfare measures, *Applied Economics* **23**, 1725–31

Lopez, R A, Shah, F A, and Altobello, M A, 1994 Amenity benefits and the optimal allocation of land, *Land Economics* **70** (1), 53–62

Luzar, E J, Hotvedt, J E, and Gan, C, 1992 Economic valuation of deer hunting on Louisiana public land: a travel cost analysis, *Journal of Leisure Research* **24** (2), 99–113

Maani, S A, and Kask, S B, 1991 Risk and information: a hedonic price study in the New Zealand housing market, *Economic Record* 7, 227–36

Mackenzie, J, 1992 Evaluating recreational trip attributes and travel time via cojoint analysis, *Journal of Leisure Research* **24** (2), 171–84

Mackenzie, J, 1993 A comparison of contingent preference models, *American Journal of Agricultural Economics* **75**, 593–603

Mackey, B G, Nix, H A, Hutchinson, M F, and Fleming, P M, 1988 Assessing the representativeness of places for conservation reservation and heritage listing, *Environmental Management* **12** (4), 501–14

Magnussen, K, 1991 Valuation of reduced water pollution using the contingent valuation method — methodology and empirical results, paper presented to the Second Annual Meeting of the European Association of Environmental and Resource Economists, Stockholm

Mäler, K-G, 1991 National accounts and environmental resources, *Environmental and Resource Economics* **1**, 1–15

Marcus, D 1995 Estate management schemes: a feudal hangover? *Estates Gazette, A submission to DTZ Debenham Thorpe dated 18 March 1995*, 9511, 132–3

Marson, C, and Quigley, J M, 1990 Comparing the performance of discrete choice and hedonic models in *Spatial Choices and Processes* (eds M M Fischer, P Nijkamp, and Y Y Papageorgiou), 219–46, North-Holland

Mattsson, L, and Li, C-Z, 1994a How do different forest management practices affect the non-timber value of forests? — an economic analysis, *Journal of Environmental Management* **41**, 79–88

Mattsson, L, and Li, C-Z, 1994b Sample non-response in a mail contingent valuation survey: an empirical test of the effect on value inference, *Journal of Leisure Research* **26** (2), 182–8

Maxwell, S, 1994 Valuation of rural environmental improvements using a contingent valuation methodology: a case study of the Marston Vale Community Forest Project, *Journal of Environmental Management* **41**, 385–99

McConnell, K E, 1990 Double counting in hedonic travel cost models, *Land Economics* **66** (2), 121–7

McConnell, K E, 1992a Model building and judgement: implications for benefit transfers with travel cost models, *Water Resources Research* **28** (3), 695–700

McConnell, K E, 1992b On-site time in the demand for recreation, *American Journal of Agricultural Economics* **74**, 918–25

McKeen, J R, and Revier, C F, 1990 An extension of: 'Omitting cross-price variable biases in the linear travel cost model: correcting common misperceptions', *Land Economics* **66** (4), 430–6

McLeod, P B, 1984 The demand for local amenity: a hedonic price analysis, *Environment and Planning A: International Journal of Urban and regional Research* **16** (3), 389–400

McLeod, P B, Roberts, E J, and Syme, G J, 1994 Willingness to pay for continued government service provision: the case of agricultural protection services, *Journal of Environmental Management* **40**, 1–16

McPherson, E G, 1992 Accounting for benefits and costs of urban greenspace, *Landscape and Urban Planning* **22**, 41–51

Mendelsohn, R, Hof, J, Peterson, G, and Johnson, R, 1992 Measuring recreation values with multiple destination trips, *American Journal of Agricultural Economics* **74**, 926–33

Menz, F C, and Mullen, J K, 1981 Expected encounters and willingness to pay for outdoor recreation, *Land Economics* **57** (1), 33–40

Michaels, R G, and Smith, V K, 1990 Market segmentation and valuing amenities with hedonic models: the case of hazardous waste sites, *Journal of Urban Economics* **28**, 223–42

Moorhouse, J C, and Smith, M S, 1994 The market for residential architecture: 19th century row houses in Boston's South End, *Journal of Urban Economics* **35**, 267–77

Navrud, S, 1991 Willingness to pay for preservation of species — an experiment with actual payments, paper presented to the Second Annual Meeting of the European Association of Environmental and Resource Economists, Stockholm

Neyret, R, 1992 *Le patrimoine a tout du developpment, Collection Transversales II*, Université de Lyon, Lyon

Nijkamp, P, and Bithas, K 1995 *Scenarios for sustainable cultural heritage planning*, in Coccossis and Nijkamp 1995

Nijkamp, P, 1975 A multicriteria analysis for project evaluation: economic — ecological evaluation of a land reclamation project, *Papers of the Regional Science Association*, **35**, 87–111

Nijkamp, P, 1988 Culture and region: a multidimensional evaluation of movements, *Environment and Planning B: Planning and Design*, **15** (1), 5–14

Owen, V L, and Hendon, W S, 1985 *Managerial economics for the arts*, University of Akron, Akron, Ohio

Paelinck, J H P, 1976 Qualitative multiple criteria analysis, environmental protection and multiregional development, *Papers of the Regional Science Association*, **36**, 59–74

Palmquist, R B, 1982 Measuring environmental effects on property values without hedonic regressions, *Journal of Urban Economics* **11**, 333–47

Park, T, Loomis, J B, and Creel, M, 1991 Confidence intervals for evaluating benefits estimates from dichotomous choice contingent valuation studies, *Land Economics* **67** (1), 64–73

Patin, V, 1988 *La valorisation touristique du patrimoine culturel* (The tourist value of the cultural heritage), Ministère de la Culture, Paris

Pearce, G, 1994 Conservation as a component of urban regeneration, *Regional Studies* **28** (1), 88–93

Pennington, G, Topham, N, and Ward, R, 1990 Aircraft noise and residential property values adjacent to Manchester International Airport, *Journal of Transport Economics and Policy* **24**, 49–59

PIEDA/ Department of the Environment 1995 *The impact of environmental improvements on urban regeneration*, HMSO, London

Point, P, 1991 A method for determining the economic value of water for irrigation: the shadow price of substitution, paper presented to the Second Annual Meeting of the European Association of Environmental and Resource Economists, Stockholm

Powell, J R, McClintock, C, and Allee, D J, 1991 The impact of contingent valuation information on water supply protection, paper presented to the Second Annual Meeting of the European Association of Environmental and Resource Economists, Stockholm

Prince, R, McKee, M, Ben-David, S, and Bagnoli, M, 1992 Improving the contingent valuation method: implementing the contribution game, *Journal of Environmental Economics and Management* **23**, 78–90

Punter, J V, 1991 The long term conservation programme in central Bristol, 1977–1990, *Town Planning Review* **62** (3), 341–64

Quigley, J M, 1986 The evaluation of complex urban policies: simulating the willingness to pay for the benefits of subsidy programs, *Regional Science and Urban Economics* **16**, 31–42

Rackham, J R, 1977 *Values of residential properties in urban historic districts: Georgetown, Washington DC and other selected districts*, National Trust for Historic Preservation, Washington DC

Randall, A, 1994 A difficulty with the travel cost method, *Land Economics* **70** (1), 88–96

Reiling, S D, Boyle, K J, Phillips, M L, and Anderson, M W, 1990 Temporal reliability of contingent values, *Land Economics* **66** (2), 128–34

Ribaudo, M O, and Epp, D J, 1984 The importance of sample discrimination in using the travel cost method to estimate the benefits of improved water quality, *Land Economics* **60** (4), 397–403

Richardson, H W, 1969 *Regional economics*, London

Roscelli, R, and Zorzi, F, 1990 *Valutazione di progetti di riqualificazione urbana*, in *Misurare nell'Incertezza* (ed R Roscelli), Celid, Turin

Rosen, S, 1974 Hedonic prices and implicit markets: production differentiation in pure competition, *Journal of Political Economy* **82** (1), 34–55

Saaty, T L, 1980 *The analytic hierarchy process*, New York

Salokangas, R 1995 *The reuse of industrial buildings in the centre of urban districts*, paper presented to the Council of Europe, Tampere University of Technology

Sanders, L D, Walsh, R G, and McKean, J R, 1991 Comparable estimates of the recreational value of rivers, *Water Resources Research* **27** (7), 1387–94

Scanlon, K, Edge, A, and Willmott, T, 1994 *The listing of buildings: the effect on value*, English Heritage, the Department of National Heritage, and the Royal Institution of Chartered Surveyors, London

Schaeffer, P V, and Millerick, C A, 1991 The impact of historic district designation on property values: an empirical study, *Economic Development Quarterly* **5** (4), 301–12

Schikade, D A, and Payne, J W, 1994 How people respond to contingent valuation questions: a verbal protocol analysis of willingness to pay for an environmental regulation, *Journal of Environmental Economics and Management* **26**, 88–109

Scribner, D, 1976 Historic districts as an economic asset to cities, *The Real Estate Appraiser*, **7** (12)

Silberman, J, Gerlowski, D A, and Williams, N A, 1992 Estimating existence values for users and nonusers of New Jersey beaches, *Land Economics* **68** (2), 225–36

Silberston 1994 *The value of Stonehenge*, paper presented to an international conference on the future of Stonehenge held in London by English Heritage

Slottje, D J, Scully, G W, Hirschberg, J G, and Hayes, K J, 1991 *Measuring the quality of life across countries*, Westview Press, Boulder, Colorado

Smith, P B, 1979 Conserving Charleston's architectural heritage. *Town Planning Review* **50** 459–76

Smith, P G, 1984 The costs and benefits of urban conservation and its impact on area revitalisation, unpublished MPhil. thesis, Bartlett School of Architecture, University College, London

Smith, S L J, 1989 *Tourism analysis: a handbook*, Harlow

Smith, V K, 1988 Selection and recreation demand, *American Journal of Agricultural Economics* **70**, 29–36

Smith, V K, 1990 Estimating recreation demand using the properties of the implied consumer surplus, *Land Economics* **66** (2), 111–20

Smith, V K, 1992 Arbitrary values, good causes, and premature verdicts, *Journal of Environmental Economics and Management* **22**, 71–89

Smith, V K, 1993 Welfare effects, omitted variables, and the extent of the market, *Land Economics* **69** (2), 121–31

Smith, V K, and Kaoru, Y, 1987 The hedonic travel cost model: a view from the trenches, *Land Economics* **63** (2), 179–92

Smith, V K, Palmquist, R B, and Jakus, P, 1991 Combining farrel frontier and hedonic travel cost models for valuing estuarine quality, *Review of Economics and Statistics* **63** (4), 694–9

Soucy, C, 1974 *Restauration immobilière et changement sociale*, Les Monuments Historiques de France **20**, 12–22.

Soucy, C, 1976 *Les coeurs d'îlots, évolution d'une pratique*, Les Monuments Historiques de France **22**, 33–36.

Spitalfields Historic Buildings Trust 1995. *A submission to DTZ Debenham Thorpe in September 1995*, London

Stabler, M, 1995 Research in progress on the economic and social value of conservation, in Burman, Pickard, and Taylor 1995, 33–50

Stébé, J M, 1995 *Les politiques publiques de réhabilation due logement social* (Public housing rehabilitation policy: the challenge of evaluation), 55–80 *Espaces et Sociétés* **78**

Stevens, T H, Echverria, J, Glass, R J, Hager, T, and More, T A, 1991 Measuring the existence value of wildlife: what do CVM estimates really show? *Land Economics* **67** (4), 390–400

Stevens, T H, More, T A, and Glass, R, 1994 Interpretation and temporal stability of CV bids for wildlife existence: a panel study, *Land Economics* **70** (3), 355–63

Strongh, E J, 1983 A note on the functional form of travel cost models with zones of unequal populations, *Land Economics* **59** (3), 342–49

Stynes, D J, Peterson, G L, and Rosenthal, D H, 1986 Log transformation bias in estimating travel cost models, *Land Economics* **62** (1), 94–103

Thayer, M A, 1981 Contingent valuation techniques for assessing environmental impacts: further evidence, *Journal of Environmental Economics and Management* **8**, 27–44

Thomas, A D, 1983 Planning in residential conservation areas, *Progress in Planning* **20** (3), 199–211

Touche Ross 1994 *York tourism strategy*, York City Council, York

Triplett, J E, 1986 The economic interpretation of hedonic models, *Survey of Current Business* **6** (1), 36–40

Triplett, J E, 1992 Hedonic methods in statistical agency environments: an intellectual biopsy, in *Fifty years of economic measurement: the Jubilee Conference on research in income and wealth* (eds E R Berndt and J E Triplett, J E), 207–37, University of Chicago Press, Chicago

Van Duren, A J, 1993 Changes in the attraction of Amsterdam city centre. *Built Environment* **18** (2), 123–37

Vatu, A, and Bromley, D W, 1994 Choices without prices without apologies, *Journal of Environmental Economics and Management* **26**, 129–48

Voogd, H, 1988 Multicriteria evaluation: measures, manipulation and meaning: a reply. *Environment and Planning B: Planning and Design*, **15** (1), 65–72

Whitehead, J C, 1992 *Ex ante* willingness to pay with supply and demand uncertainty: implications for valuing a sea turtle protection program, *Applied Economics* **24**, 981–8

Whitehead, J C, 1994 Item non-response in contingent valuation: should CV researchers impute values for missing independent variables?, *Journal of Leisure Research* **26** (3), 296–303

Whitehead, J C, and Bloomquist, G C, 1991 Measuring contingent values for wetlands: effects of information about related environmental goods, *Water Resources Research* **27**(10), 2523–31

Whitehead, J C, Groothius, P A and Bloomquist, G C, 1993 Testing for non-response and sample selection bias in contingent valuation, *Economics Letters* **41**, 215–20

Whitehead, J C, Hoban, T J, and Clifford, W B, 1994 Specification bias in contingent valuation from omission of relative price variables, *Southern Economic Journal* **60** (4), 995–1009

Williams, A, 1980 Conservation planning in Oporto, *Town Planning Review* **51**, 177–94

Willis, K, 1989 Option value and non-user benefits of wildlife conservation, *Journal of Rural Studies* **5** (3), 245–56

Willis, K, 1991 The recreational value of forestry commission estate in Great Britain: a Clawson-Knetsch travel cost analysis, *Scottish Journal of Political Economy* **38** (1), 58–75

Willis, K, Beale, N, Calder, N, and Freer, D, 1993 Paying for heritage: what price for Durham Cathedral?, *Countryside Change Unit Working Paper 43*, Department of Agricultural Economics and Food Marketing, University of Newcastle-upon-Tyne

Willis, K, and Garrod, G, 1990 Valuing Open Access Recreation on Inland Waterways, *Countryside Change Unit Working Paper 12*, Department of Agricultural Economics and Food Marketing, University of Newcastle-upon-Tyne

Willis, K, and Garrod, G, 1991a An individual travel cost method of evaluating forest recreation, *Journal of Agricultural Economics* **42**, 33–42

Willis, K, and Garrod, G, 1991b Landscape values: a contingent valuation approach and case study of the Yorkshire Dales National Park, *Countryside Change Unit Working Paper 21*, Department of Agricultural Economics and Food Marketing, University of Newcastle-upon-Tyne

Willis, K, and Garrod, G, 1991c Valuing open access recreation on inland waterways: on-site recreational surveys and selection effects, *Regional Studies* **25** (6), 511–24

Willis, K, and Garrod, G, 1992 Assessing the value of future landscapes, *Landscape and Urban Planning* **23**, 17–32

Willis, K, and Garrod, G, 1993a Valuing wildlife: the benefits of Wildlife Trusts, *Countryside Change Unit Working Paper 46,* Department of Agricultural Economics and Food Marketing, University of Newcastle-upon-Tyne

Willis, K, and Garrod, G, 1993b The value of waterside properties: estimating the impact of waterways and canals on property values through hedonic price models and contingent valuation methods, *Countryside Change Unit Working Paper 44,* Department of Agricultural Economics and Food Marketing, University of Newcastle-upon-Tyne

Willis, K, Garrod, G, and Dobbs, I M, 1990 The value of canals as a public good: the case of the Montgomery and Lancaster Canals, *Countryside Change Unit Working Paper 5,* Department of Agricultural Economics and Food Marketing, University of Newcastle-upon-Tyne

Willis, K, Garrod, G, Saunders, C, and Whitby, M, 1993 Assessing methodologies to value the benefits of environmentally sensitive areas, *Countryside Change Unit Working Paper 39,* Department of Agricultural Economics and Food Marketing, University of Newcastle-upon-Tyne

Wilman, E A, and Perras, J, 1989 The substitute price variable in the travel cost equation, *Canadian Journal of Agricultural Economics* **37**, 249–61

Wiltshire County Council and others, 1995 *Condor — the re-use of military sites* , a review of the reuse of redundant military bases in the UK, Europe and USA, Salisbury

Wind, M N A, 1991 Contingent valuation of forest management.. *A paper presented to he Second Annual Meeting of the European Association of Environmental and Resource Economists,* Stockholm

Xu, F, Mittelhammer, R C, and Barkley, P W, 1993 Measuring the contributions of site characteristics to the value of agricultural land, *Land Economics* **69** (4), 356–69

York Consulting Ltd, and Centre for Urban Development and Environmental Management,1993 *Calderdale inheritance: an assessment,* Department of the Environment, London

Zahedi, F, 1986 The analytic hierarchy process: a survey of the method and its application, *Interfaces* **16**, 96–108